MASTERING LEADERSHIP

THE MOUSETRAP WAY

The Proven Path
that makes you the leader
others will admire and follow

D1067189

MANOJ VASUDEVAN

International Leadership Coach
World Number 3, World Championship of Public Speaking

A BOOK IS A GIFT YOU CAN OPEN AGAIN AND AGAIN.”

GARRISON KEILLOR

This book is presented to

____

Presented by

____

Dedicated to the leader in you!

Title - "MASTERING LEADERSHIP THE MOUSETRAP WAY: Become the leader others admire and follow"

Copyright © 2016 by Manoj Vasudevan. All rights reserved.
Published by As Many Minds
www.AsManyMinds.com
For bulk orders and enquiries: books@asmanyminds.com
Co-produced by Thought Expressions www.ThoughtExpressions.com
To book the author to speak at your event, write to talk2us@thoughtexpressions.com

Art direction and design by Wee-Peng, weepengho@gmail.com
Images by Shutterstock.com and Keyframe photography (Pg.187)

First Edition: October 2015 with title "Leadership Lessons from the Mousetrap"
Global Edition: August 2016 with current title

No part of this book may be reproduced, transmitted or utilized in any form or by any means, electronic or mechanical including photocopying, recording, scanning or by any information storage and retrieval system, without prior written permission from the publishers and author. Limit of Liability/Disclaimer of Warranty: While the publisher and the author have used their best efforts in preparing this book, they make no representations or warranties with respect to the accuracy or completeness of the contents of this book, and we specifically disclaim any implied warranties or fitness for a particular purpose. The publisher and the author shall not be liable for any loss of profit or any other personal or commercial damages, including but not limited to special, incidental, consequential, or other damages.

Printed in the U.S.A.
Paperback ISBN: 978-981-11-0076-5
E-book ISBN: 978-981-11-0077-2

You are never too small to be big.
But, are you ready to lead?

PRAISE FOR LEADERSHIP LESSONS FROM THE MOUSETRAP

"Manoj once again amazes us with his journey and provides a simple, comprehensive, and powerful working model to be a great leader. Since majority of us do fall under the category of Leaders by Design, and not Leaders by Birth, this is the right book that shows us the way. The mousetrap provides an excellent perspective to beautifully bring out memorable lessons and easy to follow steps towards personal mastery and leadership.

I highly recommend this book to anyone who wishes to be a leader others will choose to follow."

BAMBANG WINARSO
Group CEO, Aszenda Global

"The story of the mousetrap is a true metaphor of today's corporate world where survival is often the mantra. The lessons drawn from the story are lucid and relate to everyday occurrences in the corporate environment. I am positive, if you follow the book's advice, it will not only enhance your personal dynamism and productivity, but it will also uplift your corporate ecosystem. Manoj creates a strategic road map for personal mastery which can help the reader become a new age Millennial Leader.

As an experienced practitioner in the leadership development profession, I would say this is the simplest yet most comprehensive tool created for students and professionals to develop their leadership capabilities. The quotes at the beginning of each chapter are in themselves nuggets of wisdom, each priceless."

SUKETU KOHLI
Senior General Manager Learning and Organisation Development, Mahindra & Mahindra Financial Services

"Leadership Lessons from the Mousetrap is a great fable that hits to the heart of business and organisational culture issues. An insightful read that gets you questioning your own leadership style embedded with practical tips that can make a positive impact on your business."

TODD HUTCHISON
Global Chairman, Peopleistic

"This book is a refreshing change from the leadership tomes penned across the ages – one that comes right from Manoj's heart derived through his myriad experiences. Many themes run through this, from the concept of accountability partners to the art of infusing ideas as against generating them. I find this book rather unconventional in approach – evocative as against prescriptive and riddled with touching metaphors leading to thoughtful conclusions. It lets the reader derive what's best for him or her. A must read for anyone wanting to improve on their approach to leadership!"

JOSEPH ALENCHERY
Vice President, Infosys

"Besides being a fun read, this book tells us in an intuitive way how we can assess, amend and improve our leadership behaviour. We can all relate to the mentioned stories, which makes it easier to carry the learnings into our professional and private lives. I personally enjoyed the "Mousetrap Pact" Exercises, giving me the opportunity to come up with specific to-do's as well as the practical tips on speaking/presentations."

DR. SANDRA FRIEDEL
Regional HR Partner, BASF

"Thank you for writing such an interesting book. I used your story for my team building event in my company and it was a roaring success. The story is simple and everyone understood the essence of your message.

Keep up the good work and look forward to your next book."

ROBERT CHEN
Director ARCC Holdings

"We invited Manoj to our Regional office for Lunch n Learn session. We walked away enlightened, enriched and energised from his talk. I received great feedback from my team members too, who received fabulous takeaways. Thanks for taking your time and sharing with us. For me, it was certainly interesting, intriguing and insightful."

PETER LEE
General Manager, Peerless Asia Pacific

"Some leaders are born but most are not and they become great through mere training, dedicated hard work and passion. The leadership lessons by Manoj in his refreshing approach of pedagogy will train a novice to become a great leader. I consider his professorial approach with exercises for each strategy to be an innovative learning approach using the simple mousetrap story. This is a real 'mousetrap' for people like me who do not have inborn talents to become a leader."

DR. KUNCHERIA P ISAAC
Vice Chancellor, APJ Abdul Kalam Technological University

"The Mousetrap way has a unique take on leadership issues and challenges and provides specific action steps to tackle those. Other than the highly practical lessons in the book, what I find refreshing is how Manoj presented these leadership lessons with a perfect blend of real life applications, inspiring anecdotes, powerful metaphors, though-provoking questions and self-discovery questions. This is an amazing book and I highly recommend that you read it."

NISHANT KASIBHATLA
Grand Master of Memory, Author of "Mind Tools For Peak Performance"

"From the day I met the enigma that is Manoj, one thing was very clear - his clarity of thought on Leadership and Personal Development! This book is a testament to how Manoj uses a simple fable to elaborate on a very profound foundation that defines true leadership. Leadership is not about titles, rather about taking ownership and initiative. It would be very simplistic to say that the book just emanates this one message - as this story can be reviewed in so many different dimensions. Are you eager to learn about these various dimensions, in a very practical and easy to understand manner? I suggest you read every lesson on leadership on this page turner!

SOUROV ROY
Regional Consulting Director, Epicor

"*The Mousetrap Way* reveals what it takes to be a successful leader today. Based on three decades of experience building service cultures in large organizations around the world, I have seen ordinary individuals take ownership of problems, galvanise teams to get things done, and become genuine role models of effective leadership. Even if you are not a *Lea•er by Birth,* you can become a *Lea•er by Design,* by following the principles in this inspiring book. The *Mousetrap Way* provides sharp insights and powerful leadership advice. Read this book, apply what you learn and your leadership journey will be uplifted and uplifting."

RON KAUFMAN
New York Times bestselling author *Uplifting Service*

FOREWORD FOR FIRST EDITION

"I am delighted to write a foreword for this book. I am a firm believer that you can become a great leader without necessarily having any innate leadership skills. There are several ordinary individuals who developed into great leaders including South Africa's Nelson Mandela and my personal favorite Sir Alex Ferguson, who from humble beginnings in his native Scotland became one of soccer's greatest managers.

What Manoj has achieved with this highly engaging and interactive book is to provide aspiring and established leaders with practical steps and actions to develop their leadership skills.

Together with his honest, candid approach, and clear sections for the reader to complete their own input and action plans, this book allows the reader to truly get fully engaged and make deliberate plans for personal mastery.

Not that I am surprised that the book is engaging. I first met Manoj when he was giving a keynote speech at a conference in Singapore and it was simply enthralling! He had a few hundred people absolutely engaged. That is exactly what he has managed to do in this excellent book as well.

This book is about real people - the kind of people we are all like. The reader immediately feels a connection, and together with practical steps the book delivers a fantastic learning opportunity.

As I read the book, I was learning from it, just like any other person who would read this book. As Manoj makes clear, it is all about what we do as individuals to develop our leadership skills. This book has inspired me to continue to do just that. Enjoy and learn!"

STEVE WALKER
CIO, Asia Pacific & Global WMS COE, DHL Supply Chain

PROLOGUE: A TRIP THAT FOUND THE MOUSETRAP

"I have been working so hard, better than everyone else at my level. But, this year I didn't get any promotion or pay raise. Why?"

"Over the past 5 years haven't we given you pay raises and new positions? Let me be honest with you. Manoj, you don't have the skills to go to the next level. You just don't have it."

I was sad, upset and disappointed. But, I wasn't furious with my boss for what he said. He was nice enough to tell me what he thought instead of making me live in a fool's paradise. That was a reality check that started me on a journey of self-discovery.

So far, I have worked in four different leadership roles in my life. Each role taught me something new about leadership.

First, I have worked in more than 10 countries around the world in various leadership capacities. Years ago I used to work for PricewaterhouseCoopers Management Consulting Services in Singapore. When I started working I was an expert in a certain domain. I got paid for my expertise. I was paid well. Then, I got pay raises. I got new positions. This went on for a while.

Then one day everything stopped. No more promotions, no more pay raises, no new positions. That is when I went to my boss and heard, "Manoj, you don't have the skills to go to the next level. You just don't have it."

Then one day someone told me that my career prospects would improve if I got a master's in business administration. So, I dipped into my savings for funds and went to study MBA at Imperial College, London. I spent 30 months and $50,000 on my MBA. The MBA taught me several new things. Still nothing changed in my career.

That's when I started to realise and take note of the skills I was really missing. It was not my degree. It was not my MBA. It was not my years of experience. What I had been lacking was the ability to connect, to communicate, to network, to lead, to sell. Since these skills give you power to excel in any field, I call these *the Power of Five.* I left my job and started my own consultancy firm with a focus on developing *the Power of Five.*

Second, I have leadership experience running three companies. I have worked in projects where the team members came from 46 different countries. That's when I became keenly aware about the challenges and opportunities of working with people who are different from me.

Third, in my role as a leadership coach I had the good fortune to work with clients who came from 27 different nationalities. I have mentored and coached people from almost all walks of life, like CEOs, senior executives, celebrities, UN diplomats, lawyers, doctors, teachers, professionals and students. They approached me for crafting strategies for various challenges they face, such as the execution of their roles, or when they have to plan for their future or communicating their ideas to others clearly, confidently, convincingly. Being a coach has been a mutually rewarding experience. As I coach I learn from my clients about their varied experiences, challenges, and stories. In those interactions, I learned a lot about how they lead, persuade and influence others.

Fourth, I am married with two children. I am the de-facto leader of the family. Well, at least I am responsible for everything that goes wrong. ☺ In this role I learned a lot about listening, ownership, being patient, the need to show empathy, and the consequences of my choices.

LEADERS BY BIRTH OR LEADERS BY DESIGN?

As a young boy growing up, I used to believe that leading people was one of the most difficult jobs in the world. Only a few blessed individuals can do that effectively. I was so wrong!

For the past 20 years, I have worked in large multinational companies in various countries, and for the past 10 years I have studied and researched the practical aspects of leadership in the corporate, political, and social arena.

The questions that gnawed at me were the following

- How does a person become a leader?
- Why are some people better leaders than others?
- Can you become a great leader whom others are eager to follow?
- What can you do to boost your leadership potential?
- How can we help our children pick up the right skills as they grow up?

Based on my research and my personal conversations with clients and other practitioners, I agree that some people are truly exceptional. They are born leaders. They are born with certain traits, gifts and talents that make them better suited for leadership. If you drop them into a group they will automatically emerge as a leader. They are what I call ***Leaders by Birth.***

Now, what if you are not a born leader? Can you become a leader too? Fortunately, the answer is yes. In fact, most leaders we know were not born leaders. They learned some skills, behaviours, and mindset that under the right circumstances, transformed them from ordinary persons to extraordinary leaders.

They are what I call ***Leaders by Design***.

THE PROBLEMS WITH LEADERSHIP TODAY

During interviews I am often asked, "What are the problems with leadership these days?" I believe leadership has three main problems:

- We have far too many bosses and too few leaders.
- Most people feel they are too small to be great.
- Those who genuinely want to become leaders do not have a game plan. Many traditional leadership training falls short in this regard, as the focus is on tactical interventions rather than a strategic transformation of mindsets.

THE GAME PLAN AND THE MOUSETRAP FOLKTALE

For years I have been toying with a dream to prepare such a game plan for my clients and for my children. A game plan that provides strategic steps that anyone can take, if they are able and willing. Several drafts of these game plans were reviewed by people working in the trenches, leading from the top, and delivering top line results. Based on several feedbacks, the game plan was further revised and updated. The more it crystallized, the more I became concerned about how to convey the leadership insights in a way that was memorable. Weeks went by. Then one day, I remembered a beautiful folktale my wise father told me when I was a child. He used to call it "The Mousetrap". The origins of the folktale are unknown, but upon reflection, I realised it completely supports the 18 strategic steps you need to take to be a leader others choose to follow. That's how I landed on the game plan.

This book provides you with that game plan comprising 18 strategic steps. The game plan is designed for both aspiring and successful leaders. If you are already a successful leader, remember to pass this game plan to your teams, friends, fans, and followers. If they implement this game plan, your team will become a force to be reckoned with. You would also start to notice that the extraordinary people you meet are knowingly or unknowingly following the 18 strategic steps.

FIVE WAYS TO GET THE BEST OUT OF THIS BOOK

1. GET AN ACCOUNTABILITY PARTNER!

We now live in the age of the internet and crowd sourcing. We have a more powerful way to learn and transform than by reading a book, no matter how good it is — ask for help. You will get the best out of this book if, at the end of every chapter, you use the questions provided to reflect upon and to solicit feedback from an accountability partner.

Your accountability partner could be someone among your peers, subordinates, superiors, mentors, or coaches. If you are a child, your accountability partner could be your parents, friends, teachers, or siblings. Letting someone help you out is the shortest way to success. You will soon notice that this collaboration and feedback is among the key leadership lessons!

My accountability partner is ______________________________

2. PREPARE YOUR MOUSETRAP PACT – STEP BY STEP!

At the end of each lesson, you will notice a section called "My Mousetrap Pact step". This is your *personal action tool* for self-assessment and concrete action. Remember to complete the corresponding Mousetrap Pact step, immediately after reading the chapter.

Each *My Mousetrap Pact* step is a section that has four parts.

Achievement: What are your current advantages with regard to this competency? What achievements are you proud of?

Assistance: What are your challenges? What help do you need?

Advice: Whom can you reach out to for assistance?

Action: What's the **one** next step you can take within the next **one** week?

As you will notice at the end of the book, this is a repetitive exercise to track your progress.

3. PREPARE YOUR LEADERSHIP DEVELOPMENT GAME PLAN

The collection of your Mousetrap Pact steps will eventually become your *personal leadership development* plan. You will read more about this as you go along.

4. MOUSETRAP RESOURCE CENTRE

One of the challenges of writing a book is that when new tools and studies emerge it's hard to inform the reader. Therefore, my team created an online resource centre as a supplement to this book, and it's available free to you as a reader. This online resource centre consists of recommended books, articles, videos, useful tools and is regularly updated. You can activate your access using the link below.

www.thoughtexpressions.com/mousetraponline

5. WATCH LEADERS IN ACTION

Observe your leadership role models. Are they following the lessons from the mousetrap? What habits and techniques can you learn and adopt?

6. DISCUSS AND DEBATE

Discuss and debate the content of this book with your friends, family and colleagues. More details are provided at the end of this book.

7. MOUSETRAP REALITY CHECK TOOL

Sometimes we need an honest reality check on ourselves to see how far we have come, where we are and what we can aim for. The Mousetrap Reality Check Tool is designed to assess where you are on your leadership journey. More details about the tool and more details on how to use the tool are available at the Mousetrap Resource Centre.

ONCE UPON A TIME...

...there lived a poor farmer. He lived in a small house, along with his wife. One day, the poor farmer bought a mousetrap.

The mouse of the house was terrified. "Oh, what should I do?" he shrieked.

He panicked and ran out into the farm where he saw the Hen, the Goat and the Cow.

He rushed to the Hen screaming, "Hen! Hen! There is a mousetrap in the house! There is a mousetrap in the house!"

The Hen said, "Mr. Mouse, I understand that this is a grave concern for you, but it is not my problem."

The Mouse rushed to the Goat and said, "Mr. Goat, Mr. Goat! There is a mousetrap in the house! There is a mousetrap in the house!"

The Goat replied, "Ho ho ho. It must be terrible for you. I am sorry to hear of your troubles, but it is not my problem."

The Mouse rushed to the Cow. In tears he whimpered, "Oh, Cow, Oh, Cow, Oh, Holy Cow, there is a mousetrap in the house. There is a mousetrap in the house!"

The Cow merely laughed. "Ha ha, have you ever heard of a cow being trapped in a mousetrap? Ha ha ha. I am sorry for you, but don't get me involved. It is not my problem."

You see, a mousetrap was in the house.

Everyone heard about it. All of them ignored it because it was not their problem.

That night there was a loud BANG! Something got trapped in the mousetrap. The farmer's wife was so happy. "Oh finally, I got that mouse!" She went to pick up the mouse.

It was pitch dark. She couldn't see what was trapped in the mousetrap.

A snake had gotten itself trapped in the mousetrap. As soon as she stooped down, the snake bit her. Upon hearing his wife cry out in pain, the farmer rushed into the kitchen with a lantern. He saw the snake and killed it, but the damage was already done.

The farmer's wife fell ill with a fever. The poor farmer didn't know what to do. He slaughtered the Hen and made chicken soup for his wife.

The mouse was relieved. He said to the Goat and the Cow, "I told you so. It is your fault."

The Goat replied in anger, "It's your fault! If there weren't a mouse, there wouldn't be a mousetrap in the house!"

"Let us get together and do something," the Mouse said. "There's nothing left to do," the Goat murmured. The Cow merely gave the Mouse a look of bovine indifference.

The next day many friends and relatives came to visit the farmer's wife. The poor farmer did not have food to feed them. So he slaughtered the Goat, and fed his guests.

Unfortunately, two days later the farmer's wife passed away. Many people came to her funeral. To meet the funeral expenses the poor farmer sold the Cow to the local butcher.

After this sad turn of events, the farmer was in a state of shock. He had aimed to kill the mouse, but in that process he lost everything he had except for his home and farm. He regretted his decision to buy the mousetrap. The farmer became sad and lonely and depressed. The depression took a toll on his life. He didn't have any interest or motivation to work. He was living in regret without rest, sleep or energy. He didn't find any purpose in his life anymore.

Three months later, the poor farmer passed away.

THE END.

What lessons can we learn from this story?

Please write your answers in this book. If you are not comfortable writing on the book with a pen, use a pencil.

TAKE FIVE MINUTES TO THINK ABOUT THE STORY AND WRITE DOWN WHAT YOU THINK ARE THE LESSONS FROM THIS STORY.

THIS IS TO ENGAGE YOUR BRAIN AND LEVERAGE YOUR INNATE CREATIVITY. YOU WILL BE GLAD YOU DID THAT. (*IF YOU READ AHEAD FOR ANSWERS IT WILL DEFEAT THE PURPOSE*).

What lessons can you derive from this story? Write them down.

Which character can you identify with? Why? Write that down.

Did any character remind you of someone you met in your life? Why? Write that down.

THE LEADERSHIP LESSONS

THE LEADERS BY DESIGN™ MODEL

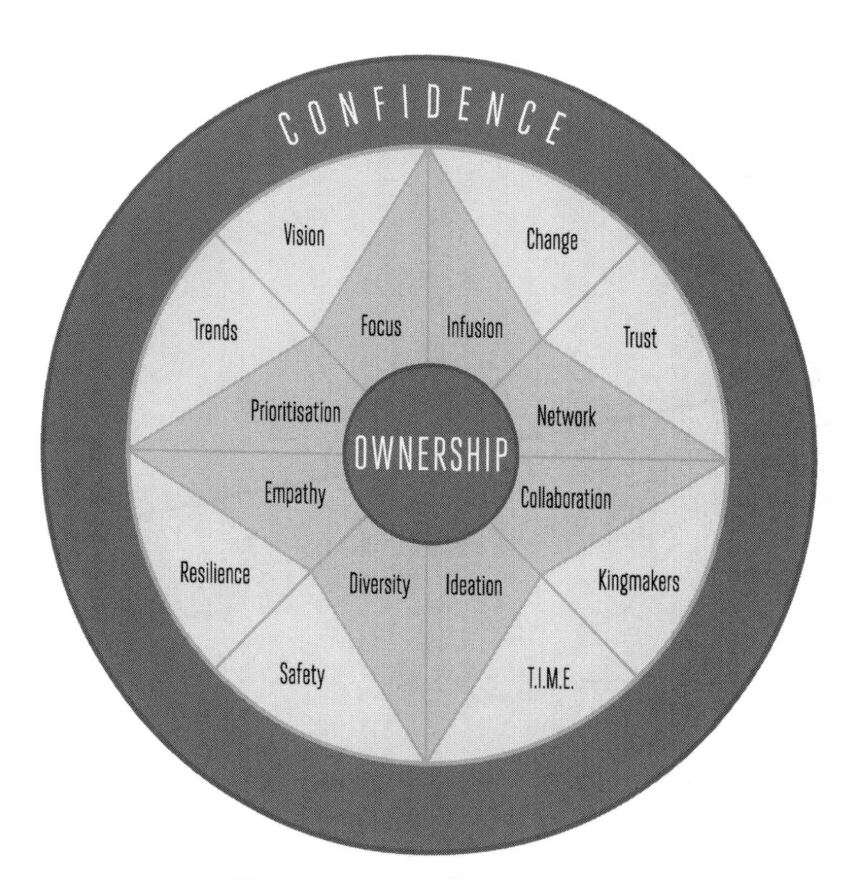

THE MOUSETRAP WAY™

CHAPTER

1

WHOSE PROBLEM IS IT ANYWAY?

Ownership is the habit that leads to leadership.”

MANOJ VASUDEVAN

FROM THE MOUSETRAP STORY:

The mousetrap didn't seem like a threat to the Hen, the Goat or the Cow. But in the end it affected all of them and the mouse was spared.

IN REAL LIFE:

Aren't such situations common in real life? In your department, organisation or team, there will always be problems. These are the mousetraps in your house. The question is - who owns those problems?

CYCLE OF BLAME, SHAME, AND COUNTERCLAIMS

Have you ever noticed how people behave when something goes wrong? Have you ever noticed how some people are inclined to blame and shame someone else for what goes wrong? Usually any attempt to blame or shame someone triggers a response of justification and counterclaims. I call this the Cycle of blame, shame, and counter claims.

Have you been a witness, victim, or perpetuator of this cycle? Who wins in the end?

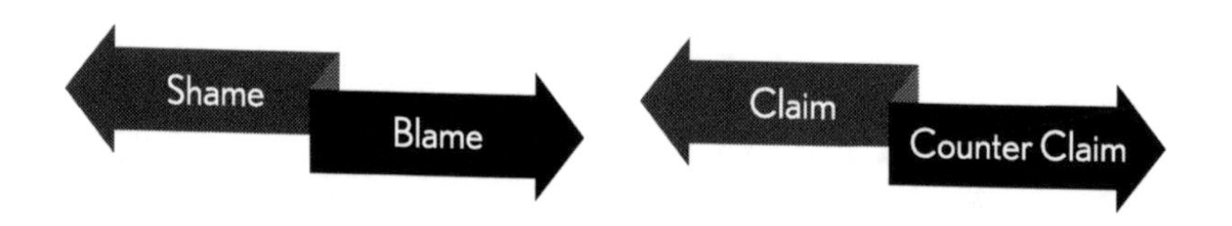

Whenever something happens somewhere, no matter how remote, insignificant, or improbable, it has a potential to affect us. Don't ignore it. Whether it is in your department, organisation or team, if something is wrong, it's not just the problem for your department, organisation, or boss. It is a problem for everyone to solve. When small errors are left unattended they can balloon into larger problems down the road. Don't ignore it because in a team somebody's problem is everybody's problem.

THE 'BROKEN CHAIR' METAPHOR

You walk into your home or office and you notice that one leg of a four-legged chair is broken. It looks safe, but it is not. Someone is going to fall and hurt themselves. What would you do? Would you walk away and expect someone else to take charge? Would you alert someone? Anyway, who's responsible if something goes wrong?

WHO SHOULD FIX THE BROKEN CHAIR?

Ownership is a habit that leads to leadership. You can be a true leader only if you are responsible and accountable for the things you ought to deliver. But the borders of responsibility do not stop at the leader's doorstep. What separates leaders from bosses is their ability to care beyond their doorstep. That doesn't mean they always have to do other people's jobs. You can inspire others by being a role model of ownership, accountability, and responsibility.

INITIATIVE WITHOUT DIRECTIVE

Those who are always waiting for directions

IN A TEAM, SOMEBODY'S PROBLEM, IS EVERYBODY'S PROBLEM.

can only be a follower, not a leader. The future looks promising for those who take initiative without directive.

WHY IS IT IMPORTANT?

The willingness to step outside your comfort zone and take responsibility not only stretches your potential, but also increases your value to whichever organisation you are associated with. In fact, you don't need a title to be a leader; the best leaders are those who are willing to take ownership irrespective of their titles.

OWNERSHIP THAT LED TO LEADERSHIP

A long, long time ago, there lived a lawyer in South Africa. He was highly educated. But he was also shy, reserved, and soft-spoken. The first time he had an opportunity to speak in court he was a disaster. As soon as he stood up to speak, his mind sat down. His legs started to shake, his breath became heavy, and he became so confused that he sat down in defeat. Thereafter, he started to expend his efforts on settling disputes out of court. Soon he became wealthy.

One night, while he was travelling on a first-class railway, a railway officer came to his cabin.

"You can't sit here. Get out!".

"Why not? I have a first-class ticket?" the lawyer said.

"No, you can't sit here. Get out!" the railway officer said.

"Why not?" the lawyer asked again.

"This compartment is for whites only. Get out!"

The lawyer was thrown out of the train in the middle of the night. As he spent the frosty night in the railway station, the cold of the winter seeped into his bones and he decided to stand up for his rights and for the rights of his fellowmen. The name of that lawyer was Gandhi.

At that point Gandhi didn't hold any high office or wasn't a member of any political party. However, after that moment of truth, Gandhi got involved in the freedom movement against British colonial rule. He felt he had to get involved without expecting someone else to fix the system. Gandhi transformed from a shy, reserved, nervous person to become a leader of 400 million people. He became a leader who is respected worldwide to this date, decades after his death.

Ownership is at the core of leaders whom others admire and follow. To be seen as a person with leadership potential, you need to build a reputation for having a keen sense of ownership. Otherwise, you will not be seen as a leader material – no matter what your designation says. After all, it's not a designation that defines a leader.

Most people are not willing or ready to take ownership. Followers expect leaders to lead by example. Be willing to take ownership and encourage others to do the same. My personal slogan on ownership is this: *Don't give excuses. Give excellence.*

THE MOUSETRAP WAY

The Mousetrap Way to leadership is to look at problems as opportunities to unlock your potential and grow as a leader whom, others will admire and follow. This is a proven path taken by all the great leaders, whether knowingly or unknowingly. On that path, ownership is the first milestone. As you will notice in upcoming chapters, ownership is necessary but not sufficient.

OWNERSHIP QUESTIONNAIRE:

How do you rate yourself on Ownership?

Amateur 1 2 3 4 5 6 7 8 9 10 Awesome

How do others rate you? (Use Mousetrap Reality Check Tool)

Amateur 1 2 3 4 5 6 7 8 9 10 Awesome

List the top five things you are accountable for:

____

____

____

____

____

What suggestions have you received regarding your level of ownership?

____

____

What can you do differently to demonstrate your sense of ownership?

MY MOUSETRAP PACT

STEP #1: OWNERSHIP

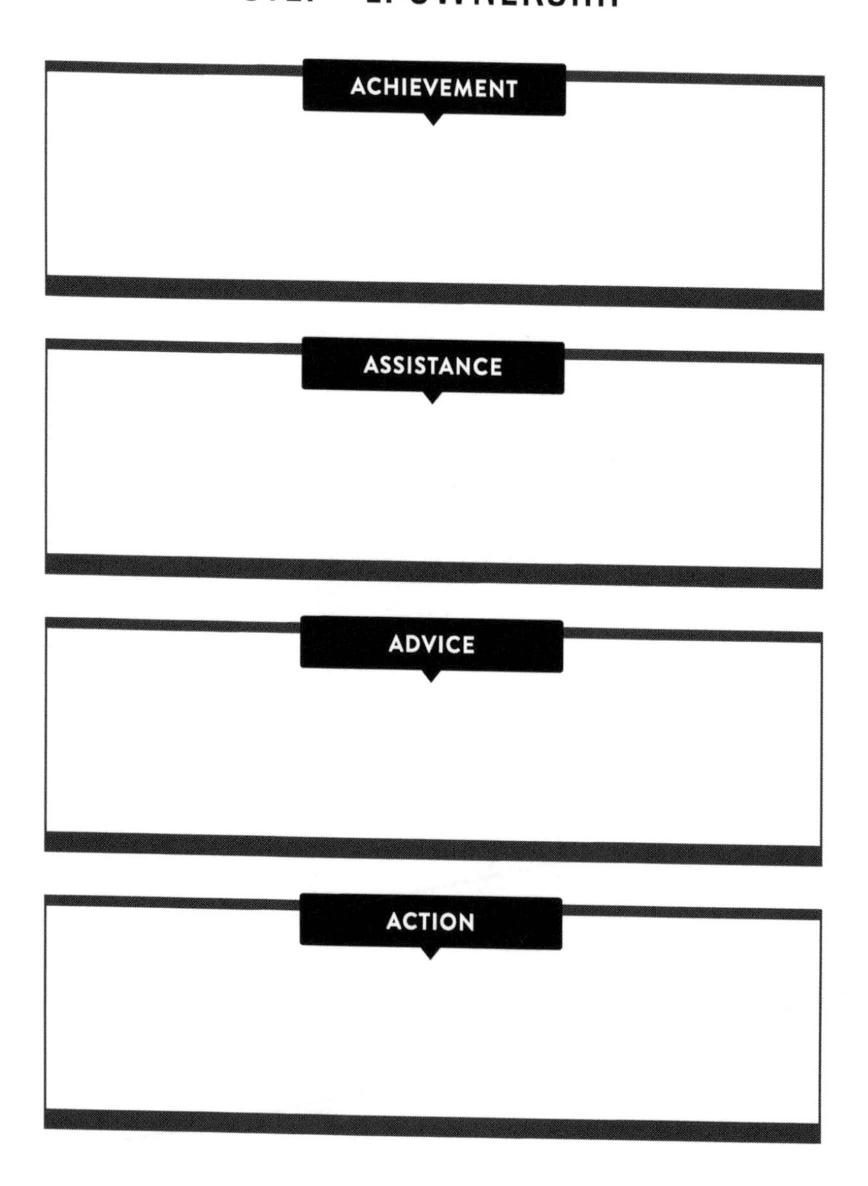

COMPETENCE IS IMPORTANT. CONFIDENCE IS PARAMOUNT.

The person with greater confidence has the upper hand.”

MANOJ VASUDEVAN

FROM THE MOUSETRAP STORY:

What did the mouse do when he saw the mousetrap? He panicked. What could he have done differently?

IN REAL LIFE:

As a leader, if you panic in times of crisis, no one would want to be near you. In fact, everyone would want to avoid you!

A time of crisis is not a time to panic. It is a time to be calm! When you communicate in panic, you communicate your panic.

COMPETENCE IRONY:

Many people who are competent in terms of skills, talents and experience get stuck in life because they lack confidence. Remember – competence is important, but confidence is paramount. In any social interaction the person with greater confidence has the upper hand. Apparently, the term 'upper hand' originates from the ancient sport of arm wrestling. The person who wins has his hand on top of the loser's hand. He has the upper hand. Similarly, if you need to have the upper hand in your leadership sport, you need to demonstrate more confidence.

A TIME OF CRISIS IS NOT A TIME TO PANIC. IT IS A TIME TO BE CALM! WHEN YOU COMMUNICATE IN PANIC, YOU COMMUNICATE YOUR PANIC.

SEVEN QUALITIES THAT INCREASE WITH CONFIDENCE:

1. Courage
2. Calmness of mind

3. Clarity of thoughts
4. Initiative without directive
5. Ability to handle adversity
6. Decisiveness
7. Speed of action

If you look at history, most of the great leaders we admire today didn't have all the required competence when they started. Still they got involved in various causes just because they felt they had to. The more they became involved, the more confident they became. The more confident they became, the more competent they became. The wait for perfect competence can be eternal. Get started with the confidence that the competence will follow.

CONFIDENCE VS ARROGANCE

People ask me, "What's the difference between confidence and arrogance?" Arrogance is characterised by excessive selfishness and indifference to others, their opinions or significance. The rule of thumb is this: Arrogance is the belief that I can do anything. Confidence is the belief that I can do this thing.

CONFIDENCE KICK-START SCRIPT

Confidence is the progressive realisation of one's capabilities. While your past experiences, fears, and insecurities can have an impact on your confidence, they shouldn't be holding you back. Lack of confidence originates from poor self-image. Find ways to boost your self-image, and your confidence will start to grow. People look up to those who project confidence in the way they talk, walk, and behave.

Write down the things that are right about you, things that are great about you and the great things people have said about you. It doesn't have to be a lot or significant. However, it has to be true, personal and positive. Read this *Confidence kick-start script* everyday as many times as you need to remind yourself of your positive traits and accomplishments. Are you letting your achievements and nice things that happen to you go unnoticed? When nice things happen to you, remember to add them to your script. Your script will grow as your confidence grows. This will slowly but surely boost your self-image and transform a competent you to a competent and confident you. Your behaviour begins to change according to your beliefs. One technique that I find useful is to read my confidence script, record it on my phone and listen to it a few times in the morning or when I need a boost.

Why is this important? If you don't believe in yourself, no one else will. Self-confidence is a skill and like all skills, you can pick this up too.

If you need help with crafting your *Confidence kick-start script,* check out the Mousetrap Resource Centre.
www.thoughtexpressions.com/mousetraponline

THE 'CAKE' METAPHOR AND A CLARION CALL FOR LEADERS

Nobody will follow you if you are not confident. You need to have the confidence that your cause is significant, that your talent is sufficient, that your time has come! Most people dream of getting the top positions in their organisations but don't work towards or stay prepared to take on those positions.

If you keep waiting for the right opportunity, the right experience, the right time, your time might never come. Others would have taken your cake and eaten it too. We need to develop the confidence to do what's right, not just what's popular.

IF YOU KEEP WAITING, SOMEONE ELSE WOULD HAVE TAKEN YOUR CAKE AND EATEN IT TOO.

A common problem in our society is that many people with competence have no confidence to speak up and stand out. On the other hand, many people without competence seem to have all the confidence. Leaders are *not* those who have no fear and self-doubt, they feel the same fear and doubt we feel and still decide to do what needs to be done.

Have you been giving up your share of cake, because you were not confident to take your share?

Be bold. Be confident. Be decisive. That's essential.

WHAT ARE WE REALLY AFRAID OF?

Marianne Williamson in her book *Return to Love and a Gift of Change* says it best: *"Our deepest fear is not that we are inadequate. Our deepest fear is that we are powerful beyond measure. It is our light, not our darkness that most frightens us. We ask ourselves, "Who am I to be brilliant, gorgeous, talented, and fabulous?" Actually who are you not to be? ...As we let our light shine we unconsciously give other people permission to do the same. As we are liberated from our own fear, our presence automatically liberates others."*

That's an essential lesson for leadership. People are more likely to follow those who act with confidence.

CONFIDENCE QUESTIONNAIRE:

How do you rate yourself on Confidence?

Amateur 1 2 3 4 5 6 7 8 9 10 Awesome

How do others rate you? (Use Mousetrap Reality Check Tool)

Amateur 1 2 3 4 5 6 7 8 9 10 Awesome

Is there something that's holding you back and affecting your confidence? What is that?

____

____

____

____

What do you think you can do to improve your level of confidence?

____

____

____

____

____

What can you do differently to demonstrate your improved level of confidence?

____

____

____

____

Can you see any issues in your team, organization or society that you could get involved to resolve? What are they?

____

____

____

____

____

MY MOUSETRAP PACT

STEP #2: CONFIDENCE

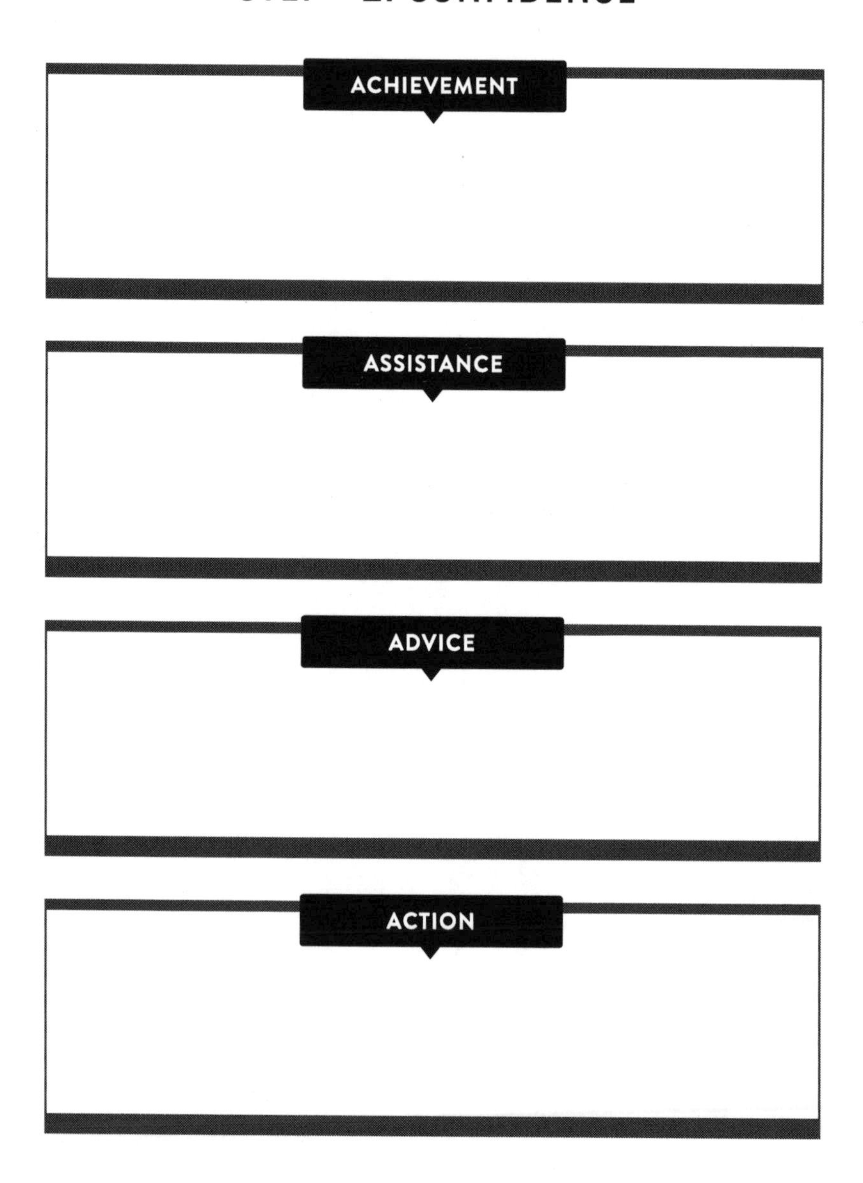

CHAPTER 3

IDEAS INFUSION!

Generating ideas isn't enough. Infuse ideas.”

MANOJ VASUDEVAN

FROM THE MOUSETRAP STORY:

Not only did the mouse panic, he was also running around yelling for help. Would he have convinced the other animals better if he had sold the idea that getting involved was in their own best interests?

IN REAL LIFE:

We live in a world where employee engagement is at its lowest ebb. It seems hard to communicate and influence the thinking of others. This is an essential skill for leaders and something you too can master.

You have three ways to communicate:

- You can tell (Works at times. Might need repetition).
- You can yell (Negative outcome in the long run).
- You can sell (Best outcome with least resistance).

Great leaders sell their ideas, vision, and plan of action. This inspires others to follow their lead and act on their behalf.

A key role of a leader is to infuse his/her ideas in their followers' minds so that they become ambassadors of the idea. It's not just about generation of visions and ideas; it is about infusing those ideas and making them contagious in a positive way so that people are stirred to act!

Great leaders know people won't buy their ideas unless they package it well and sell it well.

A FISHY TALE

A client of mine once told me about an incident at his company in the electronics industry.

A candidate was being interviewed for a research and development manager role. The candidate's experience didn't match the requirements for the job, but he had done some unrelated research on the dynamics of the movement of fish. His research topic had nothing to do with the job for which he had applied. He spoke with passion for about 20 minutes on movements of fish and got hired. The point is this. In general, people who can communicate well are perceived to be far more valuable than those who cannot. The good news is, this is a skill we can all learn.

WHAT TO NOTE WHEN YOU SPEAK:

- Be aware of what you say, how you say it and what you are doing when you say it.
- The content, sincerity, knowledge, and conviction of your conversation affect whether or not your message will be accepted.
- Your expressions, gestures, movement, and tone of voice should be in tune with what you are trying to convey. A nice thing said in a wrong tone can end in disaster.
- Structure your conversations in a way that is easy to understand and appealing to your listener's personal interests (see Infusion points below)
- Simple words are the most persuasive. Be sincere and authentic in your conversations, the tone, and body language usually follows.

HOW TO INFUSE IDEAS

- Understand infusion points and parameters of persuasion
- Paint a picture to inspire action
- Make only those promises you can keep

INFUSION POINTS AND PARAMETERS OF PERSUASION

Do you know what persuades people to change their view points? During our studies of hundreds of leadership communications, marketing campaigns and negotiation case studies, my team and I found there are several commonalities in various persuasion scenarios. During my leadership coaching sessions, I asked my clients to do research in their teams to validate our findings. Here's what we found.

Everyone in the world has at least one of the six Infusion points that, when tactfully nudged, appeals to their emotion and stirs them to action. Here are the six Infusion points

1. Pleasure
2. Profit
3. Power
4. Productivity
5. Prestige
6. Purpose

Along with the six Infusion points, two broad categories of motives exist by which people are persuaded to act:

- The prospect of gain
- The avoidance of pain

When we combine the six Infusion points and the two motives we have 12 parameters of persuasion to experiment with.

6 Infusion points X 2 motives = 12 parameters of persuasion

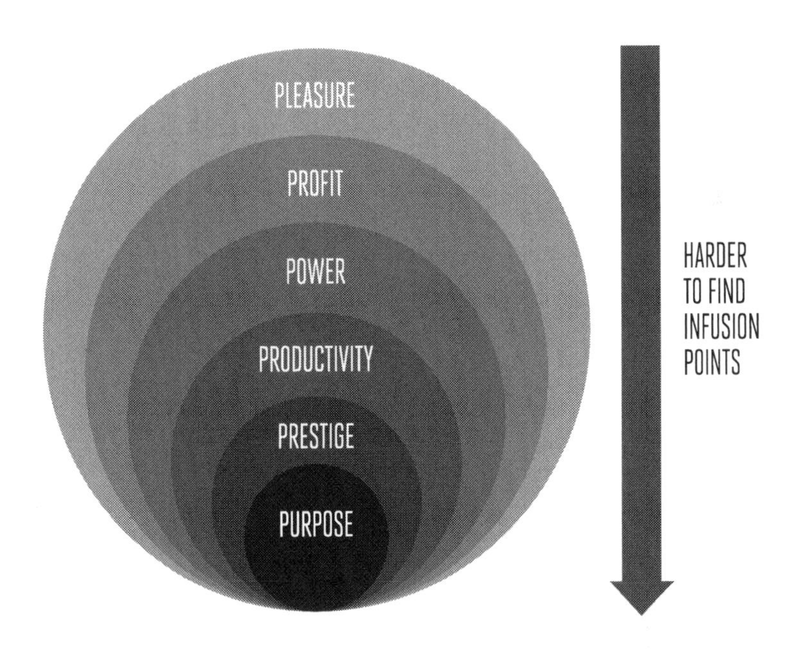

In other words, if you can discover the Infusion points of a person, you can appeal to the corresponding motive that nudges him to act. The person acts because it is consistent with what he values. For example, you can persuade a person to act by convincing him that the action is in line with his purpose in life. The converse is also true. For example, someone who is driven by a motive of increasing his profit will be motivated not only by a prospect for profit, but also by his objective to avoid loss. In some cases, the avoidance of loss is more appealing than the prospect of gain.

LEADERS INSPIRE ACTION BOSSES DEMAND COMPLIANCE

Of the six Infusion Points which is the most powerful? The most powerful and hardest to reach infusion point is Purpose. If you can connect with a person's purpose (meaning/calling) in life, they can even work for you for free. If that's hard to believe, look at the millions of people who do volunteer work (not just for charitable causes). In many cases, the volunteers spend money from their own pockets on top of their time and effort. In a way, it seems like they are *paying to work.* Of course, they don't see it that way – as the effort is aligned with their purpose or provides them a gratification that money or fame cannot bring.

Here is the key challenge and opportunity for a leader – convey ideas in a way that resonates with the Infusion points of others, who will then become willing followers.

PAINTING A PICTURE TO INSPIRE ACTION

Many clients often ask me, "Do you have a process you use to inspire your audience?" There are several processes to achieve the same purpose (For detailed tips check out *52 PRIME tips* at *www.ThoughtExpressions.com*).

Here is one easy-to-use three-step process you can use to inspire your team to take action. Most bosses ignore this need of their teams and end up conveying ideas that do not resonate.

The three-step process I have devised is the NOW-WOW-HOW™

process. This is how you structure your conversation when you want to paint a picture to convince others about your vision for the future and the action they need to take.

NOW

What needs to change? Why? Look at the current situation and find out what's lacking. Convey this to your team using the following guidelines.

- What are their needs? Connect with their needs. Remind them about their fears and goals by appealing to the relevant Infusion Points.
- What stories and anecdotes can you tell to prove your points? Make them feel and understand that doing nothing can lead to undesirable consequences.
- Convince them about
    - What are we *lacking* NOW
    - What is *blocking* us?
    - What is *blin•ing* us?

WOW

What are the possible results of the desired action? What's attractive about that? Convey the result (*Promise• Lan•*) in a way that helps them to visualize the desired result.

- Tell them about the attractive end result we will get (WOW) when your idea is adopted. You haven't told the idea yet. That will come later.

- Elaborate on the benefits of end results (WOW).
    - What do we get in our *Promised Land*?
    - The benefits need to appeal to their needs, assuage their fears or help them achieve their goals. Appeal to relevant Infusion Points to remind them about the prospect of gain and avoidance of pain.
- Give them time to let that imagination sink in.

HOW

What are the actions we need to take as a team? Convey the desired action steps in a way that looks practical, important and achievable.

- The team needs to know the way (HOW) to your *promised land* (WOW).
    - What do they need to do?
    - Which path do they need to take? Show them the HOW. This is where you articulate your idea. The HOW should be clear, concise and accurate. (It does not have to be easy, but it has to be achievable).
    - Throw a subtle Challenge to them (a nudge, some motivation), so they feel the urge to give your idea a try.

That's the NOW-WOW-HOW process to inspire action.

EXAMPLES FOR NOW-WOW-HOW PROCESS.

When people ask me to provide the proof for the efficacy of the NOW-WOW-HOW process, I am tempted to share two mildly controversial examples everyone can relate to.

When we look at the spiritual, religious organizations or cults we can notice that many are already using the process to convey their ideologies. It goes something like the following.

"The current situation of not caring for the Supreme Being is causing you to have lack of peace, lack of sleep, lack of happiness. It causes greed, jealousy and anxiety. This is a road that leads to the devil and hell fire (NOW).

If you follow the gui•elines I am about to tell you, you will be put on a path to heaven, where there is 24 x 7 party, lots of foo•, lots of fun, lots of assistants and no work(WOW).

Here is what you have to do: Be nice, believe and follow the script (HOW)."

This example is given not as sarcasm, but to prove the efficacy of this process. A prerequisite here is that the person who is proposing these ideas needs to have credibility, authority and track record. Lack of trust and belief in the leader defeats this process. You will learn in an upcoming chapter how this trust is built and developed.

Here is another example. During elections many politicians use this same process.

"The current situation in this country is terrible. We don't have jobs that pay enough, our •ebts are piling up, we are worrie• about our chil•ren's future and everything else that calls for change. (NOW).

Together we can change the system and make it happen. We can have more jobs, no debts and bring sustainable prosperity to this country (WOW).

Here is what you have to do: Vote for me and my party (HOW)."

The HOW is made to look like the most simple and practical next step. Again, this works only when the leader has built credibility and people believe in his words. Once reason many politicians lose their credibility is when they overdo this process by making promises they can't keep.

MAKE ONLY THOSE PROMISES YOU CAN KEEP

The purpose of painting a picture is mainly to convey your ideas with clarity and inspire people to take action. It is important to keep the promises you make. When this doesn't happen, trust is destroyed. An upcoming chapter details steps you need to follow to build and maintain trust.

THE 'ISLAND-MAINLAND' METAPHOR

Imagine your team is stranded on an island of misery (NOW); then you show them the mainland of prosperity and opportunities (WOW). Finally, you show them the bridge to the mainland (HOW). The shorter your bridge appears, the more appealing your solution becomes and the more inspired they will be to act.

Would that work? Try it out and see for yourself. When you follow the NOW-WOW-HOW™ process, your team will be inspired to take action. Incidentally, this is also the fundamental approach of great leaders. Leaders inspire action; bosses demand compliance.

Think of this process as you prepare to get buy-in for your ideas. You will soon be pleasantly surprised with the results you get. Most bosses

THE SHORTER YOUR BRIDGE APPEARS THE MORE APPEALING YOUR SOLUTION BECOMES.

do not follow these steps and wonder why they can't inspire their teams. As you prepare to paint the WOW situation, remember the six Infusion Points and the twelve parameters of persuasion.

SPREADING A VISION

The CEO of a multinational bank told me this, "Every time our bank recruits a new Managing Director, I will let the Human Resources department do all the process of interviewing and recruitment. When the candidate finally comes to me, I talk to him or her and transfer my vision for the organisation from my head to his or her head. I want to ensure that my vision and their vision should be exactly the same. Thereafter, they become the ambassadors of that vision."

A key role of leadership is to spread the vision. Strategies for ideas infusion will be helpful here.

A leader needs to address these six Infusion points as he or she crafts the vision and conveys his or her ideas. In general, the Infusion point that is nearest to reach is Pleasure and the Infusion point that is farthest to reach is Purpose. The reason for such distinction is this: most people you encounter may not have found out their purpose in life. Therefore, it is harder for you to know and appeal to their Purpose.

Even though it is difficult to know each individual's exact Infusion points, rest assured that it is definitely one of the aforementioned six. Therefore, when you sell your ideas, ensure that you articulate them by appealing to all six Infusion points. Your listeners will absorb the part that appeals to them the most. That's the shortest way to get them all, when you are addressing a group.

USING MULTIPLE INFUSION POINTS – A PERSONAL EXPERIENCE

You don't have to be in a formal role to try out nudging infusion points. Every challenge provides a hidden opportunity to develop your leadership skills.

At my home in Singapore, we used to have a domestic helper for 12 years. We were so used to having a helper that we did not have to worry about house work. She used to do all her work with excellence. Two years ago, she left our employment due to some family emergency. There we were, left without a helper for the first time in 12 years. We could not get a replacement soon enough. I was extremely busy due to my workload. My wife Sindu was busy with running her business. Our kids were 9 and 10 then – they were so used to having a helper at home to cook, to wash, to clean and to find their misplaced toys.

When we asked our children to assist with housework they were reluctant, saying, "That's not our job."

That's when I realised I had to take a different approach. See how I used more than one Infusion points to stir my children to action below. I am sharing this for illustrative purposes, but it is not difficult to see how you can use this in any communication.

My wife and I sat down with the kids and showed them the big picture. Firstly, I appointed my son as the head of safety and security (Prestige). I said, *"Son, you need to ensure our house is safe. Lock all doors, switch off all lights, close and lock all windows, watch out for anything unsafe–fix anything that can cause slips, trips, falls."*

He felt important and took over that job. Later I would appoint him as head of household hygiene (Prestige) and he would take charge of Garbage disposal.

Then I spoke to both my son and daughter and said, *"We humans nee• to eat to live, that's important. But most people never learn to cook their own food. If you learn to cook the dishes you like, you can be in any corner of the world and still eat the food you enjoy the most. You won't eat unhealthy food and fall sick. You will save lots of money!"* (Prestige, Pleasure, Productivity, Profit). That triggered their curiosity and developed their interest and enthusiasm in cooking. They started to help out in the kitchen with the hope that they'll learn useful life skills.

One by one, the tasks were divided between the four of us in the family — cooking, laundry, cleaning and ironing. I was also assigned the task no-one wanted to do – cleaning the dishes and tidying up the kitchen. Everyone worked with great interest and motivation. It was challenging at first, but after one week, everything was in order. By the second week, we realized we could carry on without a new helper and could have saved a lot of money earlier simply by knowing how to tap into each individual's Infusion points. The kids too learnt new habits of self-reliance.

When you are confronted with a challenge to convince others to your point of view, think of how to convey your ideas in a way that appeals to multiple infusion points.

STICKY NOTE ON INFUSING IDEAS:

- As a leader, help your team see the big picture.
- Help them see the consequences of their choices.
- Help them see the value of their efforts.
- Translate the problem in a way that will stir others to action.
- Don't just give your team tasks to do; aim to make them see the picture you believe in.

For more practical tips on infusing ideas check out the 52 tips to Persuade, Resonate, Inspire, Mesmerise and Entertain (*52 PRIME Tips*) at *www.ThoughtExpressions.com*

INFUSION QUESTIONNAIRE:

How do you rate yourself on Infusion?

Amateur 1 2 3 4 5 6 7 8 9 10 Awesome

How do others rate you? (Use Mousetrap Reality Check Tool)

Amateur 1 2 3 4 5 6 7 8 9 10 Awesome

What do you think are your personal challenges in getting others to accept your ideas and viewpoints?

____

____

____

____

What can you do to improve your ability to 'sell' your ideas and viewpoints?

____

____

____

Where can you apply the NOW-WOW-HOW process?

____

____

____

____

MY MOUSETRAP PACT

STEP #3: INFUSION

ACHIEVEMENT

ASSISTANCE

ADVICE

ACTION

INVEST NOW, HARVEST LATER

Dig your wells and build your bridges long before you need them.”

MANOJ VASUDEVAN

FROM THE MOUSETRAP STORY:

Why didn't the other animals care for the mouse? One possibility is that the mouse hadn't invested quality time to cultivate reciprocal relationships with the other animals. They didn't bother to offer help because they had no personal bond with him that made them inclined to help.

FROM REAL LIFE:

Imagine you haven't called someone you know for a very long time. One fine morning you decide to call her. What will she think? Could she be thinking you are calling only because you need help? How inclined will she be to offer help?

Leadership is built on a network of relationships. You need to build your network one link at a time and make it a habit. You will need the support of others in times of need. Therefore, it is essential to build the necessary networks that will help you out of tight corners. Ironically, this should not be your primary objective for building networks. The easiest way to build your network is to give. Give your time, effort or resources to help others. Giving is the beginning of sustainable reciprocal relationships. The tag line of a leading networking organisation, BNI International, is "*Givers gain*".

LEADERSHIP IS BUILT ON A NETWORK OF RELATIONSHIPS YOU NEED TO BUILD YOUR NETWORK ONE LINK AT A TIME AND MAKE IT A HABIT.

Adam Grant, the author of *Give and Take,*

says, "*If we create networks with the sole intention of getting something, we won't succeed. We can't pursue the benefits of networks; the benefits ensue from investments in meaningful activities and relationships.*"

It is an investment that pays back in the long run.

INVEST IN A NETWORK OF RELATIONSHIPS

A common mistake most people make is that they spend time building relationships only with people who matter. This makes them chase people who are established, significant or powerful. They ignore everybody else. You need to remember to treat everyone with due respect. You have to build amicable relationships with your supervisors, subordinates, peers, partners and anybody you can.

To put it bluntly – building relationships is all about – invest now, harvest later. We won't know which direction help is going to come from in the future. Building relationships might use up our time, money and effort. There is no guarantee that people will help us when we need their help. Still invest in those relationships because when you need to reach out to people for support, you are not dealing with strangers.

When dealing with people, a rule of thumb to follow is to stay focussed on the relationship not the transaction. Separate the person from his position and connect with the person.

HOW RELATIONSHIPS SAVED AN ORGANISATION FROM BANKRUPTCY

When I told a coaching client about the need to build lasting relationships, he in turn narrated an amazing story.

"Many years ago I was working on a project involving implementation of a new technology solution. A week before the project was expected to complete, we realised we could not deliver what we had promised. We had product issues, knowledge gaps, and testing delays.

"The day before the system was expected to go operational, my boss and I walked into the steering committee meeting with our customer's leadership team. My boss told them with a straight face, *'Sorry, but we cannot make the system operational by tomorrow'*. I was expecting an argument leading into a debate on contracts, legal terms and millions of dollars of loss, even bankruptcy. To my utter surprise, the boss from the customer's side said calmly, *'If we can't do it by tomorrow, just tell us when we can do it. We will work together to resolve the issues.'*

"I was shocked. Why didn't the customer get angry with us? Now I know why it worked that way. My boss had already built the trust and relationship long before it helped him." We need to first invest in building relationships with others and nurture those relationships long before they can support us in times of need.

This idea and the importance of investing in meaningful activities and relationships is summarised in the 'Well' metaphor.

THE 'WELL' METAPHOR

There is a saying, "The best time to dig a well is long before you get thirsty." We can't just sit around expecting to get help whenever we need it. We have to plan for that by investing in a network of relationships that we maintain and nurture. There is another saying, "Don't build walls; build bridges." In short, remember to dig your wells and build your bridges long before you need them. This will come in handy during times of crisis.

DIG YOUR WELLS AND BUILD YOUR BRIDGES LONG BEFORE YOU NEED THEM.

It may not appear easy for you to socialise and network. That's the same for almost everyone. Susan Roane, author of the bestseller *How to Work a Room*, says, "*Walking into a room full of people, especially strangers, is daunting for 90% of adults.*"

Here is the thing. Start where you are but keep moving forward to build sustainable reciprocal friendships and partnerships. You will need them sooner or later. Avoid getting into situations where you are thirsty and there is no well nearby. Don't let yourself get stranded, thirsty and helpless in a lonely island of misery.

NETWORK QUESTIONNAIRE:

How do you rate yourself on Network?

Amateur 1 2 3 4 5 6 7 8 9 10 Awesome

How do others rate you? (Use Mousetrap Reality Check Tool)

Amateur 1 2 3 4 5 6 7 8 9 10 Awesome

What do you think your challenges are in expanding your personal and professional networks?

____

____

____

____

What do you think you can do to improve your ability to network and build reciprocal relationships?

____

____

____

____

What do other people suggest you can do to improve this skill?

____

____

____

____

MY MOUSETRAP PACT

STEP #4: NETWORK

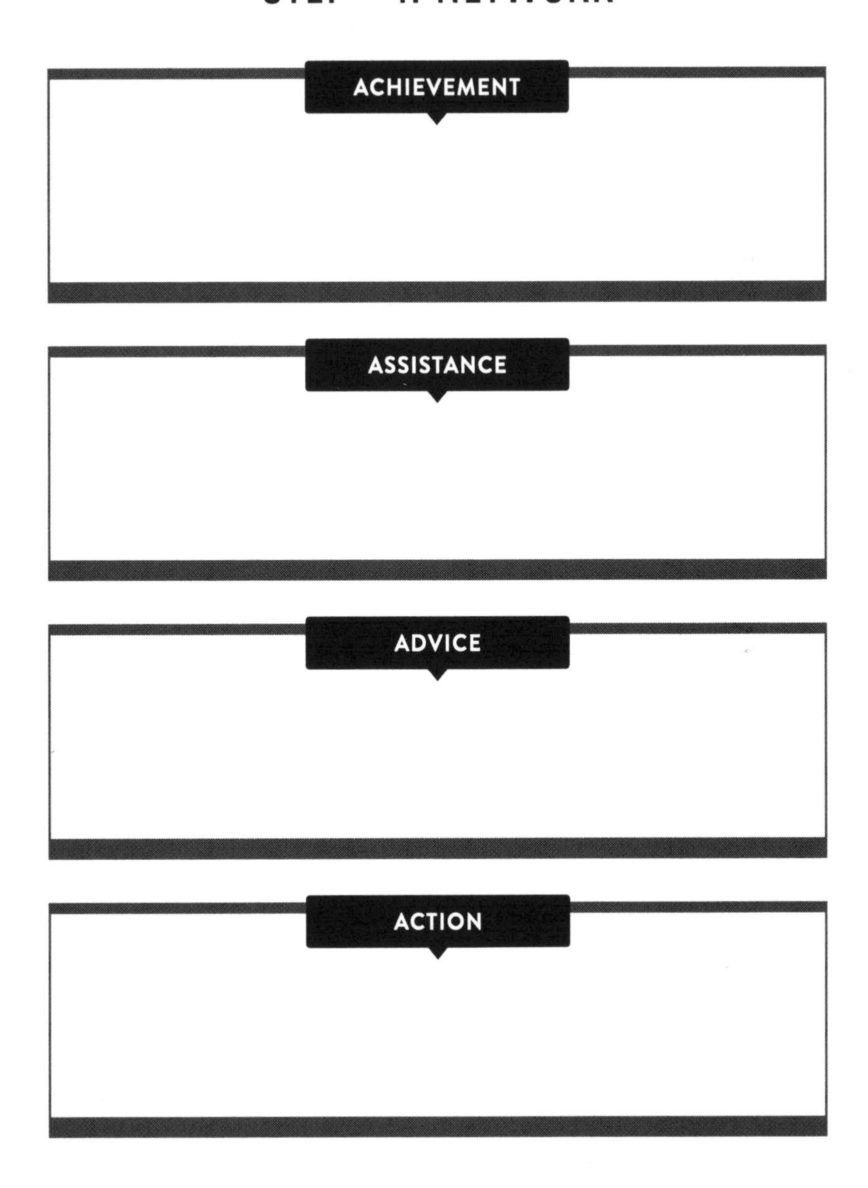

COLLABORATION IS COMMON SENSE

Tolerate. Cooperate. Operate.”

MANOJ VASUDEVAN

FROM THE MOUSETRAP STORY:

If the Hen, the Goat and the Cow had chosen to collaborate, they could have avoided their misery. It was common sense to help each other and work together. But, that didn't happen.

FROM REAL LIFE:

Collaboration is common sense. Haven't we heard so many times that the team is stronger than the individual? United we stand; divided we fall. Collaboration is common sense, but collaboration is not common. However, every successful leader understands the importance of collaboration.

THE 'TEAM OF RIVALS' METAPHOR:

The book titled *Team of Rivals,* by Doris Kearns Goodwin, provides an interesting metaphor for collaboration. The book highlights the collaborative genius of Abraham Lincoln.

RECKLESS COMPETITION DAMAGES THE COLLABORATIVE SPIRIT THAT IS ESSENTIAL FOR EXPLORATION, INNOVATION, AND EXECUTION.

In 1860, when Abraham Lincoln was campaigning to be nominated as the Republican presidential candidate, his rivals hounded him. They believed he didn't deserve to be the president. In the end, Lincoln did become the president. But on becoming the president he ignored all past rivalry. In fact, he invited some of his top rivals to join his cabinet. Lincoln seems to have believed, as many of the greatest leaders do, we don't have to agree with a person completely to work with them. When there

YOU DON'T HAVE TO AGREE WITH A PERSON COMPLETELY TO WORK WITH THEM.

are shared goals and complementary competencies, you can even collaborate with your rivals.

Years later, in 2008 when Barack Obama became the US president, he invited his top rival, Hillary Clinton, to work with him to execute his agenda for America's future. They have been working closely together since then. Despite our political leanings, we can see this as an example of how we can collaborate for a shared goal, despite past rivalries.

FOUR KEYS TO COLLABORATION

It is becoming increasingly difficult to work without collaborating with someone else. But it is often not easy to collaborate as we will face barriers.

The keys to collaboration are four-fold

- Understand the importance of collaboration

- Find the barriers to collaboration
- Lower the barriers to collaboration
- Reward collaborative behaviour

In certain instances, of course, collaboration is not ideal. For example, in an emergency situation where information is patchy, someone has to take the lead without directive. In those cases you will need to move with confidence and act decisively to resolve the crisis. Almost all other situations call for collaborative traits.

Sometimes schools and colleges inadvertently instil competitive traits that could be detrimental to a student's leadership potential. Reckless competition damages the collaborative spirit that is essential for exploration, innovation, and execution.

As a leader you need to ensure that your team maintains a collaborative spirit, irrespective of whether or not everyone agrees with each other. Even in the midst of disagreements, take the lead to find out areas of agreement, and appeal to the motives for collaboration.

If you were to take an audit of your life so far, what would you see? Have you been competing most of the time or have you been actively seeking collaboration?

COLLABORATION QUESTIONNAIRE:

How do you rate yourself on Collaboration?

Amateur 1 2 3 4 5 6 7 8 9 10 Awesome

How do others rate you? (Use Mousetrap Reality Check Tool)
Amateur 1 2 3 4 5 6 7 8 9 10 Awesome

Write down the top three instances where working collaboratively helped you achieve desired outcomes. What were the root causes?

____

____

____

____

____

____

Write down three instances in your organisation where competitive behaviour led to a wasting of resources? What was the root cause?

____

____

____

____

____

____

What do you think are the barriers to collaboration in your team or organisation?

What can be done to cultivate or boost the collaborative spirit?

MY MOUSETRAP PACT

STEP #5: COLLABORATION

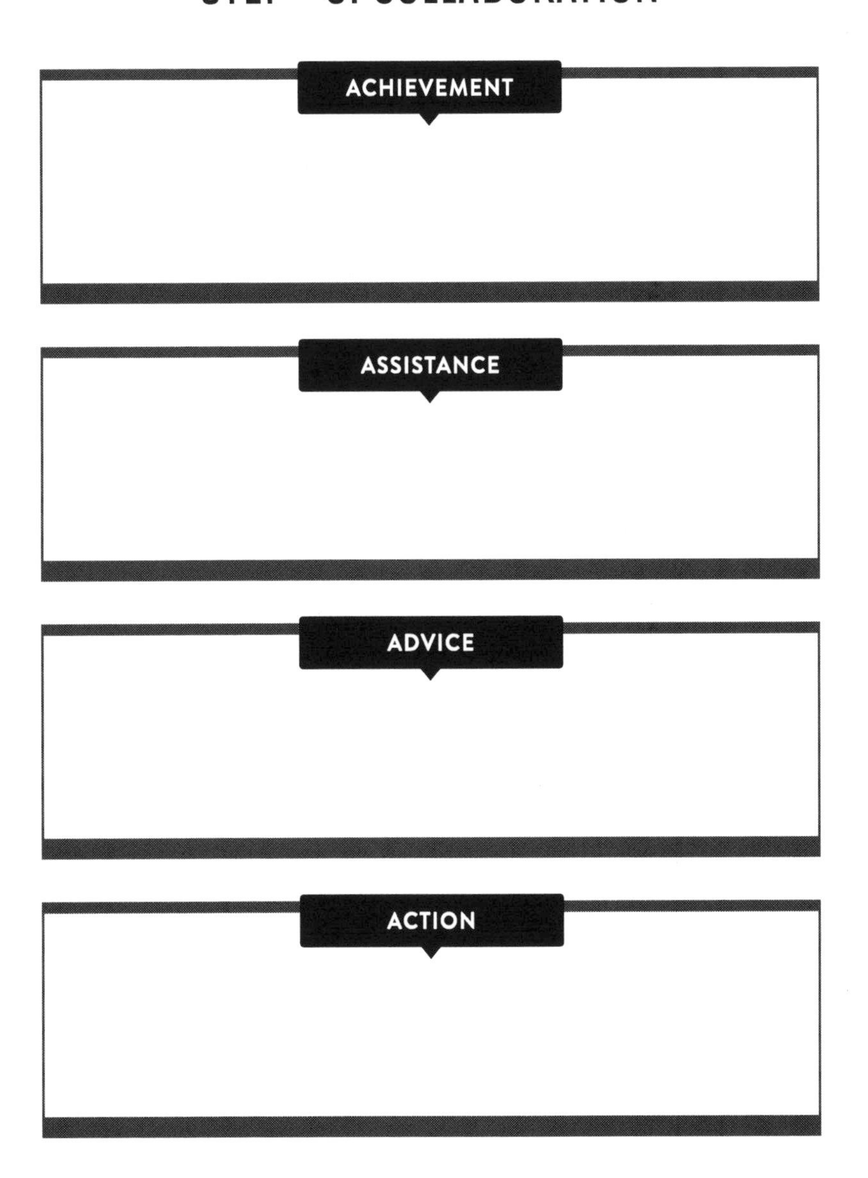

THINK OUTSIDE YOUR BRAIN

Ideation is the foundation of creation.”

MANOJ VASUDEVAN

FROM THE MOUSETRAP STORY:

During our leadership development programs, I ask the participants about how the Hen, the Goat or the Cow could have helped the mouse. The participants get into groups of four, discuss and debate and quickly come up with very creative and implementable ideas. The point is this — ideation and brainstorming are essential to generate the best creative ideas.

FROM REAL LIFE:

If you are looking for creative solutions, you can't be relying solely on your brain power. You need to think outside of your brain. Strive to reach out to others for ideas.

AS MANY MINDS AS POSSIBLE

The best companies in the modern world realise the importance of ideation. In fact, some companies specialise solely in ideation.

IF YOU ARE LOOKING FOR CREATIVE SOLUTIONS, YOU CAN'T BE RELYING SOLELY ON YOUR BRAIN.

Stanford University has a School for Design Thinking. The main objective is to get teams to come up with ideas through a process of structured questioning that challenges assumptions. This is followed by building prototypes and validating them with real users. The team would go back to the drawing board with new information or insights to start the process again. This progressive, cyclical process rapidly reduces the time taken to come up with creative solutions for challenging problems. Innovative companies like Apple and Google rely on such processes to expedite the creative process.

There are also other approaches for ideation, including Appreciative inquiry and Brainstorming sessions. I call these team ideation activities, *Collaborative Creativity*. The result is a factory generating ideas and action plans.

Why should we just rely on our own knowledge, when we can tap on as many minds as possible?

INSIGHTS FROM COACHING

As a leadership coach, I often have to work with clients who come to me with challenging problems. Many times I am able to help with their challenges just by leveraging on my prior experience. The client may, however, come up with some unique challenges to which I have no prior experience. But, I have learnt that I shouldn't be ashamed to admit what I don't know. What we do then is hold facilitated brainstorming sessions with in-house teams. These sessions aim to glean ideas from multiple brains to craft innovative solutions.

LEVERAGING THE POWER OF OTHER BRAINS IS NOT A SIGN OF WEAKNESS. IT IS A SURE SIGN OF STRENGTH.

All the major companies in the world hold such brainstorming and ideation sessions. The key point here is this: leveraging the power of other brains is not a sign of weakness. It is a sure sign of strength.

THE INTELLIGENT MACHINES METAPHOR

If we follow the advances in automation and artificial intelligence, it is clear that machines will soon become smarter than humans. For many tasks, including thinking, humans will increasingly be dependent or be replaced by machines. If you find it hard to believe, you may want to follow the advances in artificial intelligence and follow futurists like Ray Kurzweil, who had in the past accurately predicted the future.

In fact, Kurzweil claims that over the next 30 years, "*the pace of change will be so astonishingly quick that we won't be able to keep up, unless we enhance our own intelligence by merging with the intelligent machines we are creating.*"

Even in such a world, the ability and willingness to leverage the power of multiple brains and perhaps intelligent machines can make you stand out. The good thing about this advancement is that we should no longer feel the pressure to know everything, even in our domain of expertise. Why not start the habit of tapping the potential of the brains around you?

WE SHOULD NO LONGER FEEL THE PRESSURE TO KNOW EVERYTHING, EVEN IN OUR DOMAIN OF EXPERTISE.

Have you been applying old solutions to new problems? Have you been assuming that you know everything or are you willing to come up with innovative solutions using a collaborative process of ideation?

IDEATION QUESTIONNAIRE:

How do you rate yourself on Ideation?

Amateur 1 2 3 4 5 6 7 8 9 10 Awesome

How do others rate you? (Use Mousetrap Reality Check Tool)

Amateur 1 2 3 4 5 6 7 8 9 10 Awesome

Write down three instances where your team was allowed to express ideas freely without fear of judgement?

____

____

____

____

Write down top three instances where you worked with others to solve a challenging problem. What did you learn about yourself in that solution process?

____

____

____

____

____

What are the barriers to ideation in your team or organisation?

____

____

____

____

____

____

What other leadership lessons can you derive from the story? What could the animals have done differently to solve their problems? You can send us your answers at mousetrap@thoughtexpressions.com If you answer is selected by the editorial panel, you will get an honourable mention in the next edition of the book

____

____

____

____

____

____

MY MOUSETRAP PACT

STEP #6: IDEATION

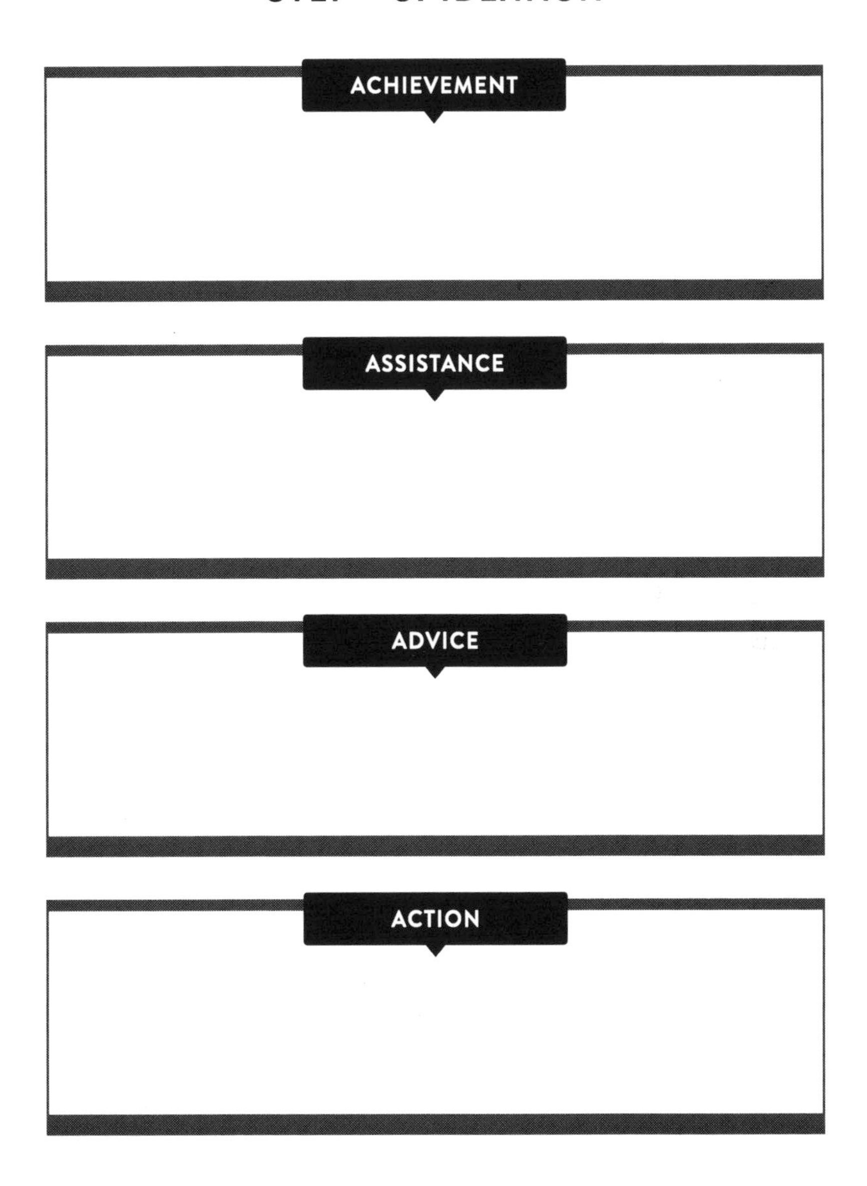

WHAT'S YOUR DQ?

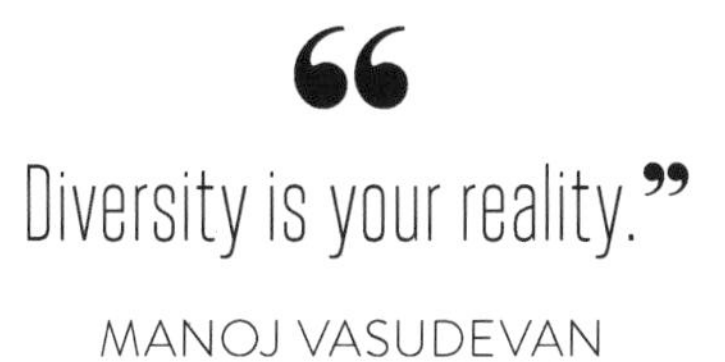

FROM THE MOUSETRAP STORY:

The Mouse, the Hen, the Goat and the Cow came from diverse backgrounds with differing skills and talents. This might seem like a hindrance to collaboration, innovation, and team work, but it is not.

FROM REAL LIFE:

I would like you to write down something. In the space provided below, write down the names of your five best friends. Exclude your relatives.

Please be truthful and write down the names now. You will be happy you followed this instruction.

Name #1: ____________________

Name #2: ____________________

Name #3: ____________________

Name #4: ____________________

Name #5: ____________________

In the list, do you have anyone who is from your home city? If yes, please strike off those names.

In the remaining list of names above, do you have anyone who is from your own race or ethnicity? **Great! Please strike off those names.**

In the remaining list of names above, do you have anyone who is of the same gender? **Fantastic! Please strike off those names.**

In the remaining list, do you have anyone who follows the same religion as you? Fabulous! **Please strike off those names.**

Count the number of names that still remain on the list.

Multiply that number by 20. That's what I call your DQ — your Diversity Quotient. This test is a quick indicator of the influences you have as you connect with new people.

If you look around your city or town you might notice the demographics have been changing. Look around and you will see more people who are different from you.

DIVERSITY IS YOUR REALITY

If you have been hoping to work with "perfect" team members, here is news for you. Such "perfect" team members do not exist. If everyone else is similar to you, you have little left to learn and leverage.

Let me use the example of Singapore to drive home a point. Being a free port and a haven for multinational companies, Singapore attracts people from almost every country in the world. Singapore has a rare cultural mix of people from all races and many different communities and cultures.

When you look at Singapore you will see different people working and living on a tiny island with an area of 719 square kilometres (278 square miles). Imagine such diversity in your city or town. Such concentration of diverse people creates challenges. Too many people in a tiny place stretch the limited resources, crowd the place and cause social anxiety.

WHETHER YOU LIKE IT OR NOT DIVERSITY IS YOUR REALITY. WHETHER YOU WANT IT OR NOT DIVERSITY IS HERE TO STAY. WE CAN'T WISH IT AWAY. IT WILL NEVER GO AWAY.

Here's the thing. This is how the world will probably look like a hundred or two hundred years from now. You will see people from different countries, cultures, and backgrounds converging in cities to work and live. Whether you like it or not, diversity is your reality. Whether you want it or not, diversity is here to stay. We can't wish it away. It will never go away.

The question is, should we keep complaining or tilt our perspective and take note of the opportunities it provides?

You see, a hundred years ago we had trade barriers. People, as well as goods and services, couldn't move across boundaries because of tariffs and restrictions. Now these trade barriers are coming down globally. You can make anything anywhere and sell anything almost anywhere in the world. Several free trade agreements exist between nations.

If you have been watching closely, yet another trend is emerging. Countries are saying to each other, *"I will allow your companies to sell their goods in my country. In return, you agree to let my people work in your companies, in your countries."*

For example, the current US-Singapore Free Trade Agreement (fta.gov.sg) reserves 5400 H1-B1 visas per year for Singaporean citizens allowing them to work in the USA, without being subject to labour market test (*the US employer does not need to prove that no other American can take the job that the Singaporean is applying for*).

This is a sign of how global trade and movements of labour are evolving around the world. Can you imagine what the scenario will be, 100 years from now?

More importantly, what does that mean to us? Globally, whether we like it or not, we will be forced to work with people who are different from us. We need to adapt. It is not a matter of tolerating diversity, nor one of only encouraging diversity, but one of embracing diversity.

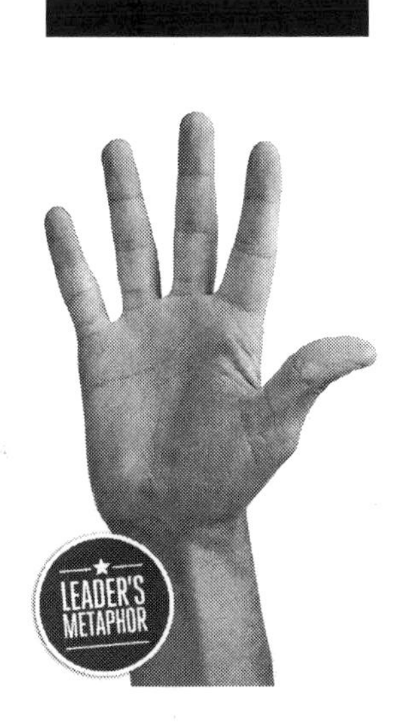

DIVERSITY IS YOUR REALITY; LEARN TO EMBRACE DIVERSITY BEFORE IT IS TOO LATE.

THE 'PALM' METAPHOR

Take a look at the palm of your hand. The five fingers of the hand are different. One is fat, one is straight, one is bent, one is long, and one is short. They have different marks, different sizes, and different shapes. A finger by itself is not strong. A finger by itself also has little meaning but if you were to clench all five fingers tightly into a fist, you will get the full power of the punch.

Likewise, we need to leverage the differing skills, knowledge and talents of various people to have the maximum impact. This will give us the edge and propel us in the path towards leadership.

Research by one of the world's leading experts on Social Psychology, Richard Crisp, provides strong evidence that by embracing diversity in our social worlds, we can awaken and maximise our creative potential.

PERSONAL NOTE ON DIVERSITY

In 2013, two Americans gave me an offer to co-author a book on public speaking. I didn't take up the offer because I always wanted to write a book myself. So, I ignored the offer and tried to write my own book. Over the next three months, I kept trying to complete the chapters. That was when I realised writing a book was not easy and I had no prior experience. Three months later, the same opportunity to co-author the book appeared again.

This time I immediately agreed to be a co-author. Soon I became part of a team of people from 12 different countries. They brought the expertise, the publisher, and the marketer. Within few weeks, we had a book that became the Amazon #1 bestseller in the public speaking category. I couldn't have done it alone. I could do it only because I decided to work with people who were different from me. That gave me the experience to complete my own books later. Since then, in all areas of my personal and professional life, I actively seek out differing perspectives to ensure I am on the right track and growing as an individual.

INCREASING YOUR DQ

Are you willing to befriend someone who is different from you? Look around for opportunities to meet new people from diverse backgrounds, cultures, and perspectives.

What if you made an effort to know a person who is different from you?

What if you made an effort to consider a different idea or perspective?

SHOULD I BECOME LIKE THEM?

The idea is not to become like others. The idea here is to be you while being willing to understand and entertain different thoughts, perspective and ideas.

What is in it for you? You will prepare yourselves for the reality and maximise your creative potential. To become a leader others will admire and follow, you need to be willing to accept people despite their differing competencies, skills and perspectives. It's no longer nice, it is necessary.

DIVERSITY QUESTIONNAIRE

How do you rate yourself on Diversity?

Amateur 1 2 3 4 5 6 7 8 9 10 Awesome

How do others rate you? (Use Mousetrap Reality Check Tool)

Amateur 1 2 3 4 5 6 7 8 9 10 Awesome

Write down the names of five individuals in your environment who are different from you in appearance, attitude, or perspectives. What is unique about them?

___

___

___

___

Write down five things you can do to improve your DQ.

___

___

___

___

___

What is the DQ of the people you work with or hang out with?

How could a higher DQ enrich your leadership potential?

MY MOUSETRAP PACT

STEP #7: DIVERSITY

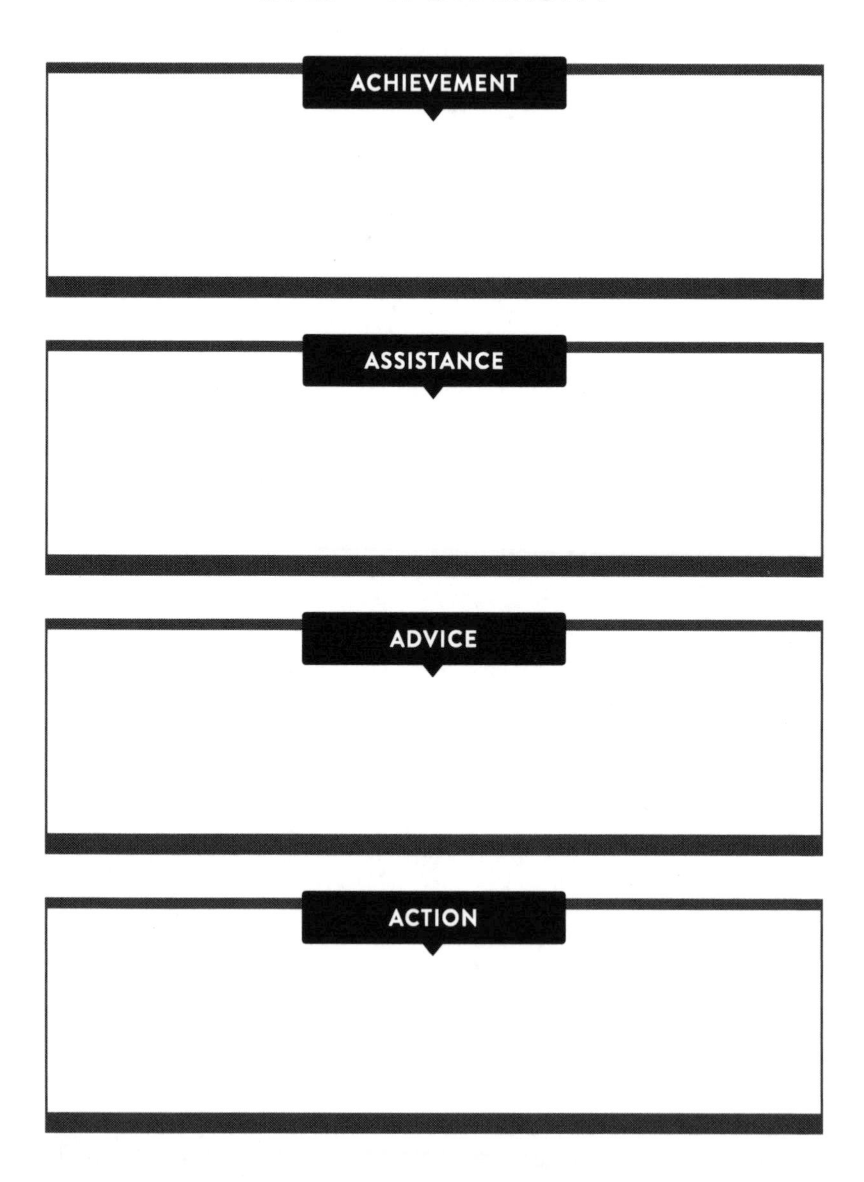

CHAPTER

8

CAN I TRY YOUR SHOES?

Ego is the enemy of empathy.”

MANOJ VASUDEVAN

FROM THE MOUSETRAP STORY:

The Hen, the Goat or the Cow showed no empathy for the mouse's anxiety and predicament. They were busy thinking about themselves.

FROM REAL LIFE:

Every sane person craves for empathy. Still, empathy is not easy to find. The ability to show empathy is an essential part of non-authoritative leadership. The celebrated American statesman and former four-star general Colin Powell reportedly said in an interview, *"I try to be empathetic, trying to see the other person's point of view. In the military, I tried to understand soldiers. In diplomatic life, when I was trying to work on a problem with a foreign minister, I would try to see what he wanted, not just what I wanted. I tried to see what we both would need."*

THE 'SHOES' METAPHOR

Showing empathy to someone doesn't mean we solve all their problems. Empathy is not about solving other people's problems.

It means we know of, care for, and acknowledge their problems, worries and concerns. In fact, we can't always solve the problem of others. But we can help them feel better and get ahead.

THE ABILITY TO SHOW EMPATHY IS AN ESSENTIAL PART OF NON-AUTHORITATIVE LEADERSHIP.

We are reliably demonstrating that we are trying to be in their shoes. Developing an attitude of empathy helps us to see from other people's perspective, which is an essential part of becoming a leader others will admire and follow.

Every leader has a healthy dose of ego. But your ego should not get in the way of your ability to empathise. Ego is the enemy of empathy.

WE CAN'T SOLVE EVERYONE'S PROBLEMS. BUT, WE CAN HELP THEM FEEL BETTER AND GET AHEAD.

FOUR STRATEGIES FOR DEMONSTRATING EMPATHY

- **Tune in**: Listening to someone is not easy. I am a poor listener by nature. But I have learnt that I need to make a sincere attempt to listen to others. Still, sometimes I feel the urge to cut the other person short and provide my opinion. Then one day I figured out a solution. To force myself to listen more during conversations, I discreetly press the tips of my left index finger and left thumb against each other. This is a cue that reminds me to listen. When I feel the urge to speak and not listen, I look at my left index finger and give it a squeeze, till it pains a bit. Over time this has helped me to listen more. When you listen, people open up, and they feel good about you and themselves. Listen. It works!
- **Judge not**: When you are listening to someone else's concerns, problems, or challenges, aim not to judge them. You perhaps have no idea what they are going through or why they are having certain opinions that are not consistent with your view of the world. Listen with the belief that they could be right until proven wrong.

- **Gossip not**: When people share their stories with you, they are putting you in a position of trust. Do not divulge their secrets to others or use that against them. If you do so, you will not only reduce your trustworthiness, but also be seen as lacking in empathy and incapable of leadership.
- **Uplift, not alienate**: When providing suggestions or giving feedback, aim to uplift the person, not alienate. Remind yourself to focus on the problem and not the person. People get defensive and hurt when they feel threatened. When there is undesirable behaviour or outcome, focus more on the possibilities of rectification than on the penalties and retribution.

In Harper Lee's book *To Kill a Mockingbird,* there is a magical line that summarises empathy. *Atticus says. 'First of all, if you can learn a simple trick, Scout, you'll get along a lot better with all kinds of folks. You never really un•erstan• a person until you consi•er things from his point of view [...] until you climb into his skin and walk around in it.'*

Empathy encourages respect and positive reciprocal behaviours. Show that you care and they will care more about you and your goals. In the words of Mary Angelou, "*I've learne• that people will forget what you sai•, people will forget what you •i•, but people will never forget how you ma•e them feel.*" Therefore, if you want others to remember, respect and follow you, remember to suppress your ego and show empathy.

EMPATHY QUESTIONNAIRE

How do you rate yourself on Empathy?

Amateur 1 2 3 4 5 6 7 8 9 10 Awesome

How do others rate you? (Use Mousetrap Reality Check Tool)
Amateur 1 2 3 4 5 6 7 8 9 10 Awesome

Write down the names of five individuals you reach out to when you need moral or emotional support. Why do you choose to go to them and not others?

____

____

____

____

____

Write down the names of five individuals who reach out to you when you need moral or emotional support. Why do they choose to come to you and not others?

____

____

____

____

____

MY MOUSETRAP PACT

STEP #8: EMPATHY

ACHIEVEMENT

ASSISTANCE

ADVICE

ACTION

WHAT SHOULD COME FIRST, THE CHICKEN OR THE EGG?

Even if you have 1000 things to do, there will only be 24 hours a day.”

MANOJ VASUDEVAN

FROM THE MOUSETRAP STORY:

Should the concern over the mousetrap have been the real priority for the mouse? He could have just avoided the mousetrap, since he knew where it was. The foremost danger for him was the prospect of being eaten by the snake. Other snakes could have been around too. His first priority should have been to protect himself from the snakes.

To a certain extent, buying the mousetrap was not a priority for the impoverished farmer. His foremost priority should have been to increase his source of livelihood.

FROM REAL LIFE:

Great leaders know their priorities. If you look around, the chances are you will see that everyone is busy. Perhaps you too are very busy. The question is, busy doing what? Are you busy doing what you are supposed to be doing, or are you busy doing something you shouldn't be doing in the first place?

PRIORITISATION SHOULD BE YOUR FIRST PRIORITY.

In the future, our world will become busier. Even with the advent of the latest cutting edge technology that is supposed to increase our productivity, we will have "less time". We will never have "more time". We will only have 24 hours a day, irrespective of the things we need to do.

Therefore, it is important to decide first what you need to be working on.

THE 'CHICKEN OR EGG' METAPHOR

Usually we hear people ask 'What came first, the Chicken or the Egg?' In our metaphor for prioritisation, Chicken and Egg represent activities we choose to do first. When it comes to prioritising your activities, ask yourself '*What **should** come first, the Chicken or the Egg?*'

WHAT SHOULD COME FIRST, THE CHICKEN OR THE EGG?

You can also think of Chicken and Egg in a different light. Chicken could represent the activities that provide you gains in the short term. Egg could represent foundational activities that prepare you to reap rewards in the future. Sometimes it is a tough choice and we have to make tough choices every day, because we only have 24 hours a day.

In his book *How to Live on 24 Hours a Day,* Arnold Bennett says *"Which of us is not saying to himself all his life: 'I shall alter that when I have a little more time'? We never shall have any more time. We have, and we have always had, all the time there is."*

Here's the thing. That book was written more than a hundred years ago. We still do not have more time, and we will not have more time in the future.

Plan your day. Remember to allocate quality time to get important things done. A senior executive of a large multinational corporation once told me that every night she would write down her plan for the next day—what she needed to do and when. She said, "*Things* •*on't always go as per my plans, but the daily planning process makes me keenly aware of my priorities. I get more things done. I do not go back to analyse how well I planned the previous day, I keep prioritising forward.*"

Don't leap into action as you get out of bed every day. Remember to plan out your day and review your plan. Otherwise you may not find time to do what's important for you.

Prioritisation is about planning to do the right things first. If you don't have a habit of prioritising, you might end up doing things you shouldn't be doing in the first place.

As you will notice in the upcoming chapters, prioritisation alone is not sufficient. However, prioritisation reminds you that your time is limited and helps you keep important tasks on your radar.

For more planning and prioritisation tips, check out the Mousetrap Resource Centre.

PRIORITISATION QUESTIONNAIRE

How do you rate yourself on Prioritisation?

Amateur 1 2 3 4 5 6 7 8 9 10 Awesome

How do others rate you? (Use Mousetrap Reality Check Tool)

Amateur 1 2 3 4 5 6 7 8 9 10 Awesome

What do you do to plan your days, weeks and months? How are you ensuring that you are doing the right things first?

Have you ever been busy doing things that shouldn't have been done in the first place? What can you do to prevent that in the future?

Let's practice. Write down your priorities for next week.

MY MOUSETRAP PACT

STEP #9: PRIORITISATION

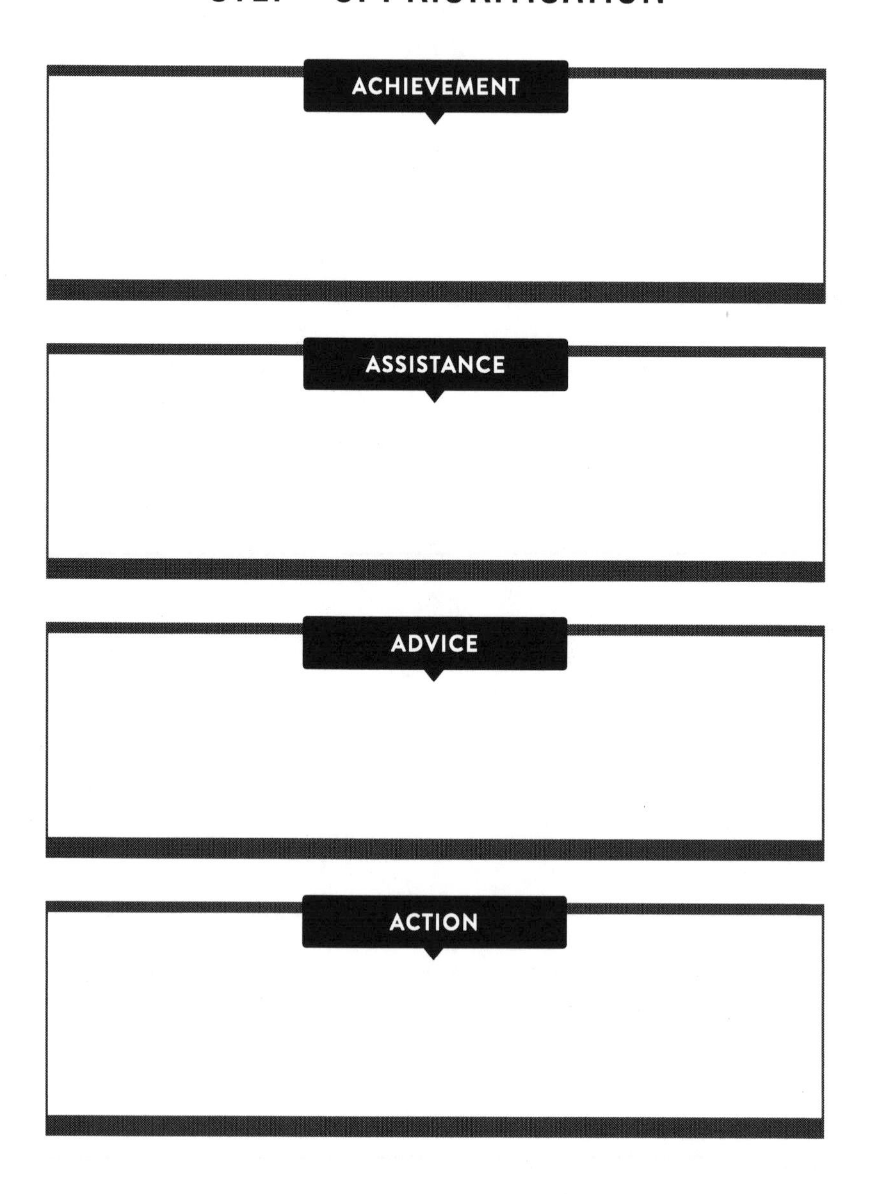

WHERE IS YOUR FOCUS?

Focus accelerates progress.”

MANOJ VASUDEVAN

FROM THE MOUSETRAP STORY:

Obviously at night the snake was out to hunt for food. But he seemed to have been distracted and was apparently fooling around with the mousetrap. What was the snake after? Why was he fooling around with the mousetrap when he should have been out hunting for food elsewhere?

FROM REAL LIFE:

Great leaders have an acute sense of focus. Have you ever set about to do something and ended up being busy doing something else? Why does that happen?

PRIORITISATION VS FOCUS

Prioritisation is planning to do the right thing first; focus is doing the right thing now.

You need to be clear on what you are after. If you are clear on what you are after, you have a higher chance of focussing your attention on that purpose. Without purpose there can be no focus. Focus accelerates progress. Absolute focus is not easily attained, but you can continually train your focus.

PRIORITIZATION IS PLANNING TO DO THE RIGHT THING FIRST; FOCUS IS DOING THE RIGHT THING NOW.

THE 'MOUNTAIN' METAPHOR

Focus is like a mountain. It is not easy to reach the top in one step. But we can gradually climb the mountain step-by-step over a period of time. Likewise we need to train our brain to focus. The secret of focus is this. The more you train yourselves to focus, the more you are able to focus at will. It takes continual effort and time, but it is very rewarding in the end. Once you can command your mind to focus at will, you will achieve a state of "flow" where you are absolutely absorbed in the task on hand. That's when you have reached the top of the mountain and height of your productivity.

THE MORE YOU TRAIN YOURSELVES TO FOCUS, THE MORE YOU ARE ABLE TO FOCUS AT WILL.

FOCUSSING ON ATTENTION

Focus is something most people are struggling with. The first step of focus is an awareness of distractions. Find out what's distracting you from the goals you set and work towards limiting those distractions.

Here are three easy-to-implement focus tips for you.

- Every time you are about to do something important, switch off all distractions like phones, social media, emails, alerts, alarms and anything else that is likely to distract you. If you are working on a computer, close all applications you don't need.
- In the middle of your work, if you get a great idea of doing something else, ignore it or make a quick note of it on your 'Do Someday' list and continue with the task on hand.

- If you are worried about missing an emergency call right when you are absorbed in your task, just delegate the handling of your calls to someone else or redirect your calls to voicemail. Other options include keeping an out-of-office message on e-mails; an I'm-busy status on your messaging applications; or a "don't disturb me now" sign on your desk. For example, I have a "Can't talk now, but I love you" status on my messaging applications. Most people respect that and will get back to me later.

Remember this: Focus accelerates progress. The more focussed you are, the more progress you would make and get energised to achieve more. This might be hard to implement at first, perhaps because you are used to attending to distractions. Now try getting used to focus.

For tools on prioritisation, focus and productivity, check out the Mousetrap Resource Centre.

FOCUS QUESTIONNAIRE

How do you rate yourself on Focus?

Amateur 1 2 3 4 5 6 7 8 9 10 Awesome

How do others rate you? (Use Mousetrap Reality Check Tool)

Amateur 1 2 3 4 5 6 7 8 9 10 Awesome

When you are doing an important task, how long can you hold your attention without distraction?

____

____

Write down the five things that usually distracts you.

____

____

____

____

____

What can you do to prevent such distractions?

____

____

____

____

____

MY MOUSETRAP PACT

STEP #10: FOCUS

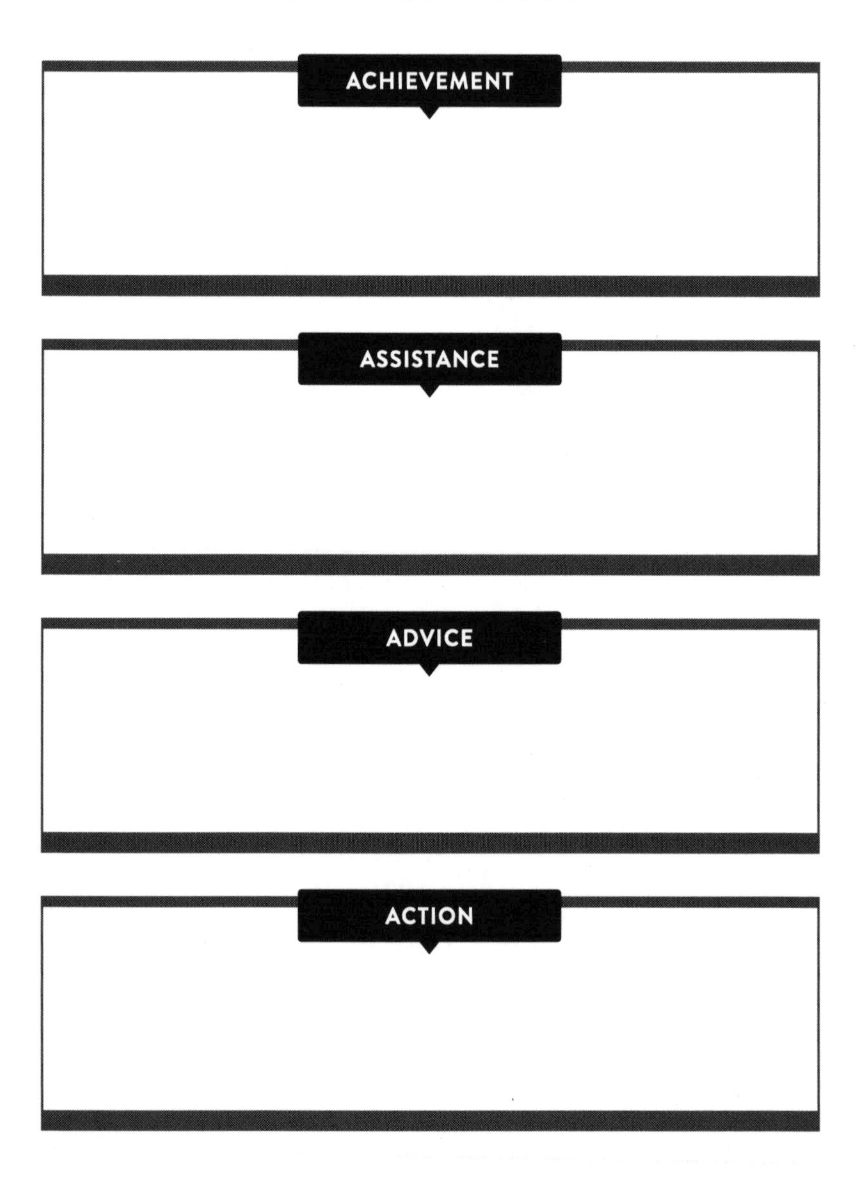

CHAPTER

11

CHANGE HAPPENS WITH FIVE CONSTANTS!

Change happens with five constants. Expect. Adapt. Adjust. Adopt. Accept.”

MANOJ VASUDEVAN

FROM THE MOUSETRAP STORY:

The bigger animals of the farm were not expecting such a rapid change and chain of events. In fact the Hen, the Goat and the Cow were treating the small mouse with a big-brother attitude. But they were not too big to fall.

FROM REAL LIFE:

You are not too big to fall. No matter how great things are going for you now, that could change without notice. Your job, position, or title is not a badge of immunity. It cannot provide you cover forever. It is very likely things will change all of a sudden and adversely affect your future.

GREAT LEADERS KNOW THAT IF YOU HAVE THE RIGHT MINDSET, CHANGE NEED NOT ALWAYS BE PAINFUL.

Great leaders know that if you have the right mindset, change need not always be painful. Here is the thing about change. Change happens with five constants. Expect. Adapt. Adjust. Adopt. Accept.

Expect: The pain of change is bad when you do not expect it.

Adapt: The pain of change is worse if you are not able to adapt to it.

Adjust: Sometimes, even in the midst of drastic changes, you get an opportunity to alter the course of the change to limit its impact on you.

Adopt: You can benefit from the change if you notice what is good in it and adopt that.

Accept: Most importantly, you need to be prepared to accept what you cannot change. For that, you need to be aware of what you can't change.

THE 'SAIL' METAPHOR

A popular proverb attributed to William Arthur Ward says it best *"The pessimist complains about the wind; the optimist expects it to change; the realist adjusts the sails"*. Great leaders develop the right mindset towards change. Even if change might surprise them, it doesn't shock them. They know change is inevitable and looks for ways to handle it. Rain or shine, stay ready to adjust the sail.

RAIN OR SHINE, STAY READY TO ADJUST THE SAIL.

WHAT CAN YOU DO AS A LEADER?

Ensure that your team understands the five constants and knows how to deal with changes. To lead a change, you need to be aware of the key principles below

- Communication is the backbone of effective change leadership. Nobody likes an unexpected disruptive change. You need to be honest and empathise with your team when you communicate change.
- Demonstrate that you are committed to carry out the change. Inspire your team and gain their commitment to partner with you to implement the change.

- Lead from the front like a commander of an army, yet keep an ear open to listen to concerns and suggestions. Be seen as a leader who is assisting others to adapt. This will reduce uncertainty, insecurity and help to keep team morale high.

DEMONSTRATE THAT YOU ARE COMMITTED TO CARRY OUT THE CHANGE.

CHANGE QUESTIONNAIRE

How do you rate yourself on Change?

Amateur 1 2 3 4 5 6 7 8 9 10 Awesome

How do others rate you? (Use Mousetrap Reality Check Tool)

Amateur 1 2 3 4 5 6 7 8 9 10 Awesome

Write down the top three things you plan to achieve in the next three months?

____

____

____

What are the three things that can disrupt any of those plans?

____

____

What preparations can you make to handle that disruption?

MY MOUSETRAP PACT

STEP #11: CHANGE

(Your attitude and flexibility towards change)

ACHIEVEMENT

ASSISTANCE

ADVICE

ACTION

BALANCE THE T-CYCLE

Trust is built by effort and demolished by stupidity.”

MANOJ VASUDEVAN

FROM THE MOUSETRAP STORY:

Even after the Hen was slaughtered, the Mouse kept alerting the other animals about the impending danger and asked them to act. Still no one listened to him. No one seemed to trust him.

FROM REAL LIFE:

Trust is the foundation of influence and leadership. We are often unsure about whom we can trust. We trust friends, family, and strangers depending on our judgements of their intent. But once their actions are not in line with their promises or are below the benchmark of our expectations, they lose our trust. Trust once lost is usually lost forever.

The converse is also true. People are consistently looking for clues about whether or not you are trustworthy.

PEOPLE ARE CONSISTENTLY LOOKING FOR CLUES ABOUT WHETHER OR NOT YOU ARE TRUSTWORTHY.

THE T-CYCLE METAPHOR

To gain the trust of others you need to know how to ride what I call the T-cycle. Imagine a bicycle. The back wheel represents who you truly are. The front wheel represents what you project yourself to be. I term this the T-Cycle. Trust is a delicate balancing act between who you are and what you project yourself to be. You need to balance this like riding a bicycle. If there is a misalignment or imbalance, you are likely to fall on your face.

Have you seen people whom you don't feel like trusting? Is that

because they give you inconsistent signals of who they are? It could be so. What is consistent is trusted. What is inconsistent is doubted.

HOW TO GET OTHERS TO TRUST YOU

I share the technique of building trust with you in the belief that you will use this for fair use and not to manipulate someone. Manipulation is not only unethical, it is counterproductive. Manipulation wouldn't sustain trust for long. Trust is built by effort and demolished by stupidity.

WHAT IS CONSISTENT IS TRUSTED. WHAT IS INCONSISTENT IS DOUBTED.

We trust people who consistently **show** character, sincerity, competence, confidence, courage, loyalty, honesty, selflessness, empathy. In other words, if you want others to trust you, you need to demonstrate the same consistently. It's really simple and straightforward if your intentions are sincere, compassionate and for mutual benefit.

9 INDICATORS OF TRUSTWORTHINESS

Take a look at the 9 indicators of trustworthiness. When you meet others they are consciously or subconsciously looking at these 9 indicators and watching out for misalignments.

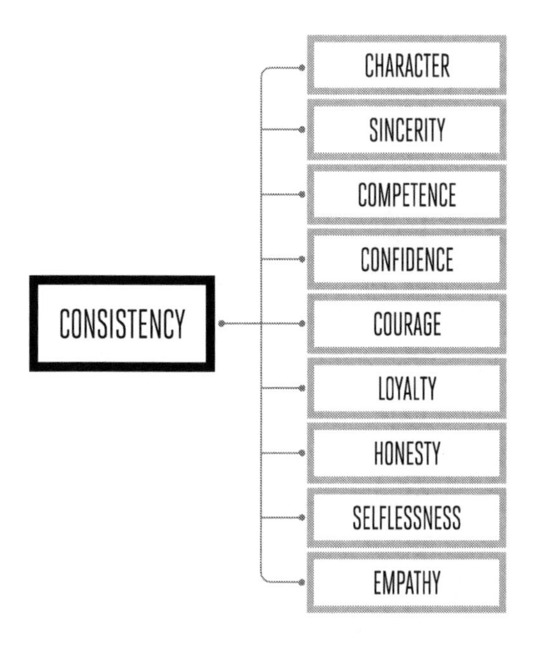

If you are seen to be consistently living your stated values and meeting the trust indicators above, you build trust. People are more willing to admire and follow those they trust.

TRUST QUESTIONNAIRE

How do you rate yourself on Trust?

Amateur 1 2 3 4 5 6 7 8 9 10 Awesome

How do others rate you? (Use Mousetrap Reality Check Tool)

Amateur 1 2 3 4 5 6 7 8 9 10 Awesome

Write down the names of five people whom you trust completely. Why do you trust them?

____

____

____

____

____

Write down the names of five people who completely trust you. Why do they trust you?

____

____

____

____

____

Write down the names of two people whom you do not feel like trusting? What makes you feel so?

____

____

MY MOUSETRAP PACT

STEP #12: TRUST

ACHIEVEMENT

ASSISTANCE

ADVICE

ACTION

WHO ARE YOUR KINGMAKERS?

Every king is surrounded by kingmakers.”

MANOJ VASUDEVAN

FROM THE MOUSETRAP STORY:

When the situation started to deteriorate quickly, the animals had no clue as to what to do. The animals didn't have mentors whom they could have gone to during the moments of crisis. They had no advisors, and that was a key contributor to their predicament.

FROM REAL LIFE:

Every king is surrounded by kingmakers. All leaders who have made their mark speak about the men and women who have served as their advisors, coaches, mentors and assistants. Who are your Kingmakers?

MENTORS CAN HELP YOU BE THE BEST YOU BY BRINGING OUT THE BEST IN YOU.

EIGHT BENEFITS OF HAVING KINGMAKERS

1. Gain new perspectives and trusted advices.
2. Have someone with whom you can share your personal and professional challenges.
3. Improve your confidence and capability to deal with adversity.
4. Get genuine constructive feedbacks for improvement.
5. Leverage on mentor's experience and network of contacts.
6. Have someone who can hold you accountable or encourage you to achieve your plans.
7. Avoid repeating past mistakes.
8. Saves the money, time and effort you might have to spend in trying to figure out solutions by yourselves.

You need to have someone to lean on and learn from, especially during a crisis. It is not only nice; it is necessary. You can find kingmakers everywhere. It can be your team members, your supervisors, advisors etc. Surround yourself with people who can help you in your cause and achieve your goals. You need to get a team and get to work. Look for the best people and look for the best in people. Develop and empower your team by entrusting them with important work.

Mentors are usually the best kingmakers. Mentors can help you be the best you by bringing out the best in you.

THE ILLUSION OF THE 'SELF-MADE' MAN

Have you encountered people who say they are self-made? I too used to take pride in the fact that I am self-made, until I was reminded by a speaker who said that no man is an island. In our life, we encounter people who guide us at critical junctures. Without them, the journey of our lives might have taken another route. Have you had such people in your life? Keep a look out for guides and mentors who can keep you on the right route.

I remember a time when I was afraid to speak in public. I tried to figure it out by myself for decades with no progress. Eventually I joined a speaking club near my place of work. Over the months I met people who gave me valuable inputs to make me a better speaker. I also started to speak outside the club and in the process met many more people and mentors.

Over the next three years or so, I would get a mentor each for humour, for storytelling, for English language, for body language, for vocal power, for executive presence, for professional speaking and the like. Within few years I was speaking at the finals of the World Championship of Public Speaking, speaking amongst the top 10 competitive speakers in the world, and I eventually won the World number three position amongst 35,000 aspirants from some 135 countries.

These days when people ask me about the secret of my quick success I look them in the eye and say, *"I am not self-made; I am mentor-made."*

Today I am a mentor and coach to many people, and I love helping others to shorten their learning curves, like the way my mentors shortened my learning curves.

THE 'RANDOM-WALK AND GUIDED-RUN' METAPHOR

Years ago, I stumbled upon an article by NASA titled "*The Ancient Sunlight*". It mentions about how Sunlight originates from the Sun's core and the long random path it has to take to reach earth. A light particle that originates at the Sun's core travels at an amazing speed of 300,000 kilometres per second. At such high speeds, we should expect the light particle to reach the Sun's surface within three seconds. However, it doesn't. It takes up to 170,000 years!

Why? After the light particle originates from the Sun's core, the particle collides with other charged particles and gets diverted. This process of collisions and diversions continues, causing the light particle to take random steps – a behaviour known as – *Random Walk*. Due to the *Random Walk,* the light particle takes 10,000 to 170,000 years, just to reach the surface of the Sun! Once the light particle reaches the Sun's outermost surface, it takes only 500 seconds to reach earth.

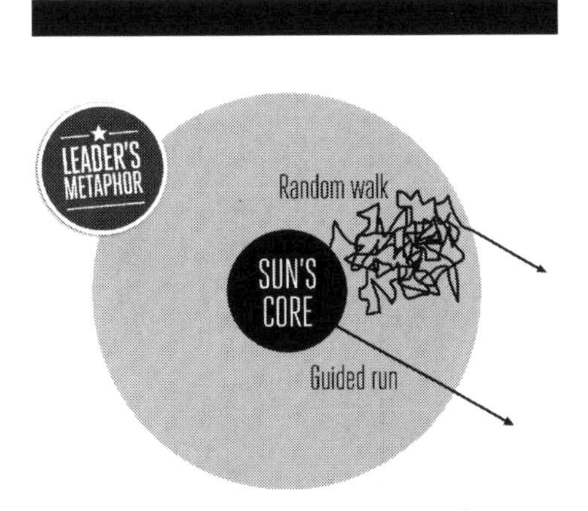

ARE YOU DOING A RANDOM WALK OR A GUIDED RUN?

This reminds us of what happens when we try to do everything by ourselves. Without kingmakers, we might be traveling on a *Random Walk* and wasting years in the process. Kingmakers can help to find shortcuts that speed up your journey. With the help of kingmakers, the *Random Walk* can become a *Guided Run*. Why take 170,000 years for doing something that can be done in three seconds? Learn to get help from kingmakers.

Who are your kingmakers? How often do you meet them?

KINGMAKERS QUESTIONNAIRE

How do you rate yourself on having kingmakers?

Amateur 1 2 3 4 5 6 7 8 9 10 Awesome

How do others rate you? (Use Mousetrap Reality Check Tool)

Amateur 1 2 3 4 5 6 7 8 9 10 Awesome

Do you have kingmakers? Who are they?

____

____

How often do you keep in touch with them?

____

____

Have you ever asked someone to be your mentor or coach? If yes, what response did you get?

____

____

Write down the names of five people, who could be your kingmakers?

____

____

____

____

____

MY MOUSETRAP PACT

STEP #13: KINGMAKERS

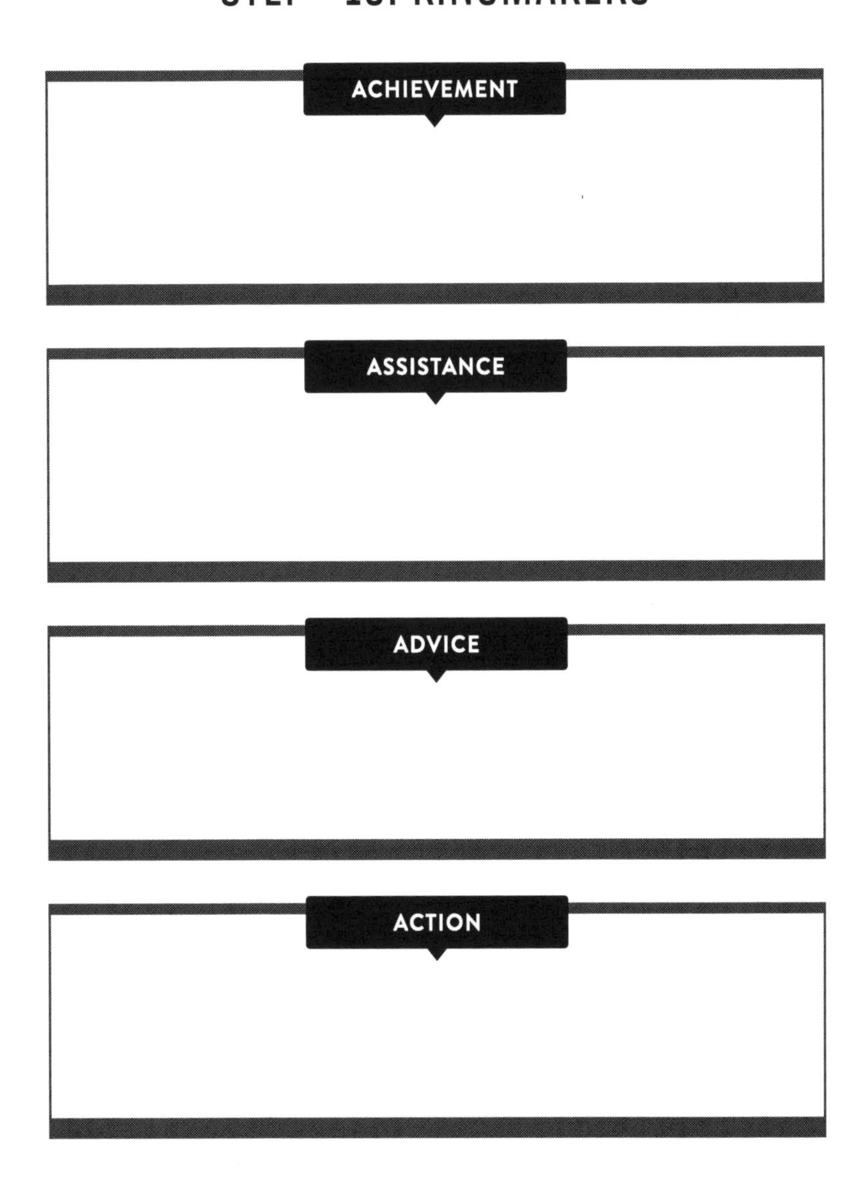

CHAPTER

14

STRETCH T.I.M.E.

Purpose provides meaning to life.”

MANOJ VASUDEVAN

FROM THE MOUSETRAP STORY:

The farmer lost his vision and purpose in life after the traumatic turn of events. The lack of vision and purpose affected his mood, behaviour, and health which eventually led to his untimely demise. Couldn't he have avoided that?

FROM REAL LIFE:

Have you seen people who struggle to have work-life balance, positive mood and motivation? Even with the right circumstances some people are less effective in this regard. This causes stress, illness, and tiredness.

Strive to stretch your T.I.M.E. – Tenacity, Interest, Motivation and Energy.

How do you stretch your T.I.M.E.?

TENACITY:

Tenacity is the determination to continue whatever you are doing in spite of obstacles. This is a source of power all great leaders develop. They don't put off until tomorrow what needs to be done today.

MAINTAIN YOUR TENACITY, INTEREST, MOTIVATION AND ENERGY.

When you feel like quitting what you are doing, keep going for a while longer. Each time you do this, it builds your tenacity. This becomes a habit. It is as if you are stretching your muscle and lifting weights to strengthen it. A positive attitude of doing whatever it takes to fulfil the promises you make, ensures that each day you live life to the fullest.

INTEREST AND MOTIVATION:

We can never have adequate discipline to do our work unless we have an interest and motivation for the work. We need to continually find ways to develop our interest and boost our motivation. Here are some tips.

1. Set goals and missions. Not just easy ones. Set some goals that seem beyond your reach. Those that put a stretch on your skills and talents. On a daily basis, remind yourself of the goals you need to work towards. This will increase your interest and motivation over time.

2. Goals you believe in give purpose to your life. These goals could be outside your scope of work or domain of expertise. All great leaders have lived a purpose-driven life. Your purpose will feed your interest and motivation.

3. You may not always get the opportunity or time to work on achieving your goals. Sometimes life gets in the way, and we are forced to do things we may not like—for example, an assignment or project you don't like to do. Try to connect what you are forced to do with what you want to do and see how it can still contribute in some way to help you achieve your goals. In his famous speech, "*Stay hungry. Stay foolish.*" Steve Jobs says "*You can't connect the dots looking forward; you can only connect them looking backwards. So you have to trust that the dots will somehow connect in your future.*" A firm belief in that wisdom will help you to see meaning in whatever you do.

ENERGY:

1. No matter what people tell us, we cannot be productive at all

times. You need to find the times in your day when you are at your productive best. Leverage on those times to do the toughest of tasks.

2. No matter how busy you are find time to rest and sleep. Billionaire businessman Richard Branson says "*We all nee• our own space an• it's goo• to pause an• •o nothing. It gives us time to think. It recharges our bodies as well as our minds.... Virgin is a worldwide company, I find I need to be awake much of the time. One of the t hings I am very goo• at is catnapping, catching an hour or two of sleep at a time. Of all the skills I have learned, that one is vital for me.*"
3. Avoid activities that drain your energy or make you gain negative energy. For example, avoid gossips and negative news like the plague. It does you little good and spoils your mood, at times for weeks. Instead, try music, videos, sports, books or do any activity that elevate your mood and make time for such hobbies and activities.
4. Be well hydrated at all times. Several researches show that adequate amount of water in our body enhances our focus, energy, and productivity. Ask your doctor about the amount of water you need to be drinking every day.

STRETCH YOUR T.I.M.E. TO GET PAST OBSTACLES.

THE 'LITTLE FLOWER' METAPHOR

The little flower that found a way to bloom

reminds us of an important fact of life. We need to stretch our T.I.M.E. to get past obstacles.

In your work or projects, there will be times of panic, disillusionment, and frustration. Those are not just challenges; those are opportunities to develop the leader in you!

Here is the question. What are you doing to manage your tenacity, interest, motivation and energy?

For more tips and suggested readings visit the Mousetrap Resource Centre.

T.I.M.E. QUESTIONNAIRE

How do you rate yourself on T.I.M.E.?
Amateur 1 2 3 4 5 6 7 8 9 10 Awesome

How do others rate you? (Use Mousetrap Reality Check Tool)
Amateur 1 2 3 4 5 6 7 8 9 10 Awesome

Write down three activities that elevate your mood? What exactly do you feel when you do those activities?

____

____

____

____

Write down three activities that lower your mood? What exactly do you feel when you do those activities?

____

____

____

Write down the five specific steps you can take to stretch your T.I.ME.

____

____

____

____

____

MY MOUSETRAP PACT

STEP #14: T.I.M.E.

(Tenacity. Interest. Motivation. Energy.)

ACHIEVEMENT

ASSISTANCE

ADVICE

ACTION

BUCKLE UP!

Safety is your best insurance policy.”

MANOJ VASUDEVAN

FROM THE MOUSETRAP STORY:

The farmer's wife went into the kitchen without taking any precaution. Despite the dark, she didn't even bring along the lantern. That triggered a chain of events that destroyed the household.

FROM REAL LIFE:

There is a proverb that says, "*Trust in God, but lock your car.*"

Leaders take risks, but they are also keenly aware of the high cost of disruptive events and therefore take safety precautions.

Safety trumps convenience.

THE 'SEAT BELT' METAPHOR

Just because something is convenient doesn't make it safe. It might be convenient not to buckle up in a plane. But if outside climatic conditions change, the aircraft can have a rapid descent. A friend of mine told me how the plane he was travelling on descended by about a hundred feet. People who did not buckle up rose and hit their heads on the luggage compartment. Some of these safety measures are in place for a reason. If you don't have a strong reason not to, buckle up!

You can't prevent all accidents, but you can notice and prevent accidents that are waiting to happen.

What safety risks are you taking in the name of convenience?

JUST BECAUSE SOMETHING IS CONVENIENT DOESN'T MAKE IT SAFE.

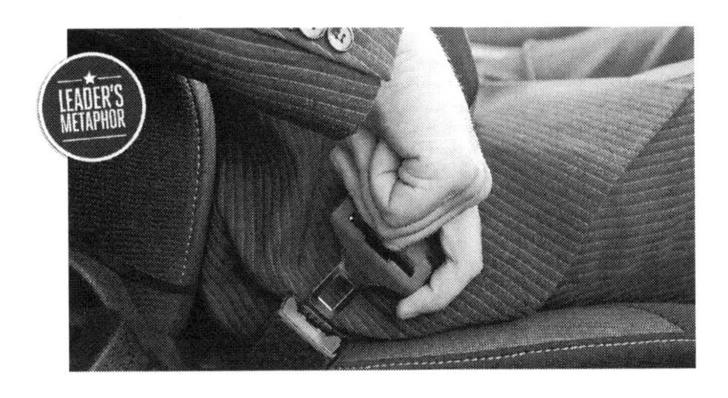

IF YOU DON'T HAVE A STRONG REASON NOT TO, BUCKLE UP!

SAFETY QUESTIONNAIRE

How do you rate yourself on Safety?

Amateur 1 2 3 4 5 6 7 8 9 10 Awesome

How do others rate you? (Use Mousetrap Reality Check Tool)

Amateur 1 2 3 4 5 6 7 8 9 10 Awesome

Take 10 minutes to think this through and do this as a mental exercise.

Do a safety-assessment of your environment. Do you notice any accidents waiting to happen?

____

____

____

If such accidents were to happen, what could be their potential cost in terms of time, effort, money and human costs?

____

____

____

____

____

In your team or organisation, is someone taking risky shortcuts in the name of speed or convenience?

____

____

____

____

____

MY MOUSETRAP PACT

STEP #15: SAFETY

ACHIEVEMENT

ASSISTANCE

ADVICE

ACTION

CHAPTER

16

YOU CAN'T ALWAYS BE RIGHT, THAT'S ALL RIGHT

Resilience is the refusal to be paralysed by failures.”

MANOJ VASUDEVAN

FROM THE MOUSETRAP STORY:

The farmer felt he had made a huge mistake by buying the mousetrap. One thing led to another and destroyed his household. He lived a life of regret. But regret didn't change anything for the better.

FROM REAL LIFE:

Every leader is bound to make mistakes. Some dwell on it. Many let go and move on. You can't always be right. That's all right. Making mistakes is an essential process of learning. Making mistakes is not a problem. Making the same mistakes repeatedly is the real problem. If you repeatedly make the same mistakes, it means you haven't been learning from them.

The only mistake is to be afraid to make more mistakes. Don't stop. In the event of an embarrassing mistake, however, quit living a life of regret. It will not change anything bad about the past, but it can destroy everything good about the future.

In his book *Lea•ing*, Alex Ferguson, who is regarded as one of the greatest and successful football managers of all time, shares a remarkable anecdote that highlights the importance of resilience. "*...I was •etermine• not to be cowe•.... For me, that whole approach to life coul• be boile• •own to the 101 seconds of injury time that it took United to turn what had looked like a 1-0 defeat by Bayern Munich in the 1999 Champions League final into a 2-1 victory. Bayern Munich's ribbons had alrea•y been attache• to the Cup in anticipation*

THE ONLY MISTAKE IS TO BE AFRAID TO MAKE MORE MISTAKES. DON'T STOP.

of the victory ceremony, an• the presi•ent of UEFA was preparing to present the trophy to them, when our refusal to give up meant those ribbons were change• to re•.... For me, the only time to give up is when you are •ea•."

Resilience is the refusal to be paralysed by failures or setbacks.

THE 'BASKETBALL' METAPHOR

I remember when I took my then eight-year-old daughter to the basketball court. She took the ball, took aim and used all her power to shoot. The ball didn't even reach the basket. I said, "*Darling, let's go back. You are short for this game.*" She looked me in the eye and said, "*No, Da••y. My next shot will be my best shot ever.*" I thought what if we took that attitude to life? Instead of focusing on the last shot, what if we focus on the next shot.

LEADER'S METAPHOR

YOUR NEXT SHOT COULD BE YOUR BEST SHOT.

Everyone has bad days. But we don't have to turn bad days into bad weeks, bad months and bad years. When you have a setback, take responsibility, learn the lessons and move on. The question is not whether or not you missed the shot. The question is, are you still in the game? Your next shot could be your best shot.

Basketball legend Michael Jordan is celebrated as one of the best basketball players of all time. This is what he had to say - "*I've misse• more than 9000 shots in my career. I've lost almost 300 games. 26 times, I've been trusted to take the game winning shot and missed. I've failed over and over an• over again in my life. An• that is why I succee•.*"

In 1985, when Steve Jobs was fired from Apple, a company he founded, it was a huge public humiliation for him. Despite the temptation to quit he chose to do what he loved to do. A few years later, he rose back to glory, and today he is a legend that continues to inspire thousands of others.

What mistakes of your past are you holding on to? Let go of the setbacks and look forward to the bounce backs. Hope is what keeps the dream alive.

RESILIENCE QUESTIONNAIRE

How do you rate yourself on Resilience?

Amateur 1 2 3 4 5 6 7 8 9 10 Awesome

How do others rate you? (Use Mousetrap Reality Check Tool)

Amateur 1 2 3 4 5 6 7 8 9 10 Awesome

What are the top three regrets in your personal/ professional life?

____

____

____

____

____

____

Were you solely responsible for what happened?

What can you do to change the state of regret?

MY MOUSETRAP PACT

STEP #16: RESILIENCE

WATCH OUT FOR THE SHADOW

Be aware of what's coming your way."

MANOJ VASUDEVAN

FROM THE MOUSETRAP STORY:

When the Hen was slaughtered, it was a clear sign for the Goat and the Cow to watch out. If they had noticed what was coming they could have been better prepared.

FROM REAL LIFE:

There is an old saying *"What goes aroun• eventually comes aroun•"*. True leaders are watching out for changes in the environment. They are aware of trends. They strive to keep themselves ahead of the rest and alert their followers in time.

THE 'SHADOW' METAPHOR

In *Lochiel's Warning,* poet Thomas Campbell writes:

"Lochiel, Lochiel, beware of the •ay!
For, dark and despairing, my sight I may seal,
But man cannot cover what Go• woul• reveal:

DO YOU SEE WHAT'S COMING YOUR WAY?

'Tis the sunset of life gives me mystical lore,
***And coming events cast their shadow before*.**"

LEADERS NEED TO KEEP AN EYE ON THE HORIZON, NOT JUST TO CHASE THE RAINBOWS, BUT TO WATCH OUT FOR THE SHADOWS OF COMING EVENTS.

We need to be aware of the potential big impact of small events. Keep an eye on changes, trends and events. We can't take everything for granted. Week after week, we hear about people falling from grace by getting caught up in avoidable situations.

Leaders need to keep an eye on the horizon, not just to chase the rainbows, but to watch out for the shadows of coming events.

We can use our eyes and ears to notice events and see trends as soon as they emerge.

If you notice a problem or trend in your team, organisation, neighbourhood, or family, you need to ask yourself three questions

- Can that problem become worse?
- What other consequences can it lead to?
- What can be done to keep it under control?

Sometimes we are so engrossed in our day-to-day tasks that we don't see what's coming our way. Watch out for what's coming your way. People admire and follow those who can alert them about the trends that might affect them.

TRENDS QUESTIONNAIRE

How do you rate yourself on Trends?

Amateur 1 2 3 4 5 6 7 8 9 10 Awesome

How do others rate you? (Use Mousetrap Reality Check Tool)

Amateur 1 2 3 4 5 6 7 8 9 10 Awesome

What trends do you see in your team or organisation that could potentially grow into a problem?

____

____

____

____

Who else is aware of this trend?

____

____

____

____

____

____

What do you think should be done?

What can you do?

MY MOUSETRAP PACT

STEP #17: TRENDS

ACHIEVEMENT

ASSISTANCE

ADVICE

ACTION

CHAPTER 18

YOU ARE NEVER TOO SMALL TO BE BIG

Size matters.
The size of your dreams matters."

MANOJ VASUDEVAN

FROM THE MOUSETRAP STORY:

Let's revisit the story once again. All characters died, except the Mouse. In the end ironically, the Mouse became the boss of the house. He lived a life of pleasure and leisure. Today someone wrote a book about him. Who could have predicted that?

FROM REAL LIFE:

The real credit to the Mouse is that he detected the mousetrap and made an attempt to alert others. Even if it seems he didn't deserve to be the boss, the fact that he became one proves a point.

Here's the point. Sometimes, some people end up in positions they never planned for, or deserve. Sometimes opportunities to lead present themselves.

Life will give you opportunities to become a leader, whether or not you deserve it. Opportunities to lead are all around us. Sometimes you get opportunities as a surprise or as a shock. In the army, if the commanding officer dies in battle, the sergeant becomes the de-facto commander.

"ALL YOUR DREAMS CAN COME TRUE IF YOU HAVE THE COURAGE TO PURSUE THEM." WALT DISNEY

You are never too small to be big. The question is, if you get an opportunity to lead, are you staying ready to take the lead and lead your team to triumph?

YOU ARE NEVER TOO SMALL TO BE BIG

Throughout history we have had examples

of improbable people becoming important leaders. The current Indian Prime Minister Narendra Modi, who is a leader of more than one billion people, started off as a boy selling tea to railway passengers. Les Brown was labelled *mentally retar•e•* and still ended up as one of the top motivational coaches in the world. Malala Yousafzai of Pakistan, stood up against violent extremists as an eloquent activist for female education. In that process she got shot, but survived to inspire millions and won the Nobel Prize. When Abraham Lincoln was a child, nobody might have looked at him and said he could become a sterling example of great leadership. Still he became one. Walt Disney, the inventor of Mickey Mouse, transformed from a struggling cartoonist to an enduring legend. He says, *"All your •reams can come true if you have the courage to pursue them."*

Every day you encounter opportunities and challenges. When the circumstances are right, the opportunity to lead and grow will present itself. Don't focus on the challenges and ignore the opportunities. As the Mousetrap story tells us, *you are never too small to be big.*

In his book Originals, Adam Grant cites scholarly research that shows *"Chil• pro•igies, it turns out, rarely go on to change the worl•. When psychologists study history's most eminent and influential people, they •iscover that many of them weren't unusually gifte• as chil•ren."*

This is an encouraging finding for us. You don't need to rely on in-born skills (*Lea•er by Birth*) to be an influential leader others will admire and follow. You can be a *Lea•er by Design* by following *The Mousetrap Way.* That is, to look at problems as opportunities to unlock your potential and grow as a leader others will admire and follow.

But as Robert Service says, "*It is later than you think.*"

IT IS LATER THAN YOU THINK

The perfect time may never arrive. For years I have been telling family, friends, and coaching clients about *The Mousetrap Way*. Several people told me to write the book, and I have been delaying it, citing various excuses. Then two years ago, while I was delivering a talk about the mousetrap story in Singapore at the Orchard Parade Hotel, I saw an elderly man furiously taking notes. After my talk he came to speak with me. His name was Mr. Lim, a retiree living in Singapore. "*Why don't you write a book on this topic?*" he asked.

"*Okay, but who reads books these days?*" I said.

"*Based on my decades of working experience,*" he said. "*I can tell you this. The lessons you shared are extremely relevant and timeless. The way you say it makes the message stick. I don't know what you want in life. All I can say is this. As you grow older, you will get weaker; you will have memory lapses; your health will start to deteriorate; your eyesight will start to fail; you will have lesser energy to write that book. It's later than you think.*"

So here it is. You are never too small to be big, but it's later than you think. Act now.

THE 'BINOCULARS' METAPHOR

What's your vision for the future? Even if it is far away, can you see it?

If you firmly believe in your vision, you can ignite your passion. When you are burning with passion, you will be committed to action. No

IF YOU FIRMLY BELIEVE IN YOUR VISION, YOU CAN IGNITE YOUR PASSION.

doubt, even when you are committed to action, you will encounter successes and failures, ups and downs, light and darkness. Still, your vision will help you to see through the darkness.

Imagine you are a leader with such awareness, belief, passion, connection, commitment, and vision that even sees through darkness. Would others choose to admire and follow you?

Remember — if you choose to emulate a role model of yours or if you want to be the leader of your tribe or if you want to start a movement, your dream is possible. Just face the challenges, be willing to demonstrate ownership, seize the opportunities and follow *The Mousetrap Way*.

What's holding you back?

VISION QUESTIONNAIRE

How do you rate yourself on Vision?

Amateur 1 2 3 4 5 6 7 8 9 10 Awesome

How do others rate you? (Use Mousetrap Reality Check Tool)

Amateur 1 2 3 4 5 6 7 8 9 10 Awesome

What plans are you making for your future?

____

____

____

____

____

When was the last time you reviewed your progress? How often do you review your progress?

____

____

____

____

____

Are you in any way setting limits to your dreams?

MY MOUSETRAP PACT

STEP #18: VISION

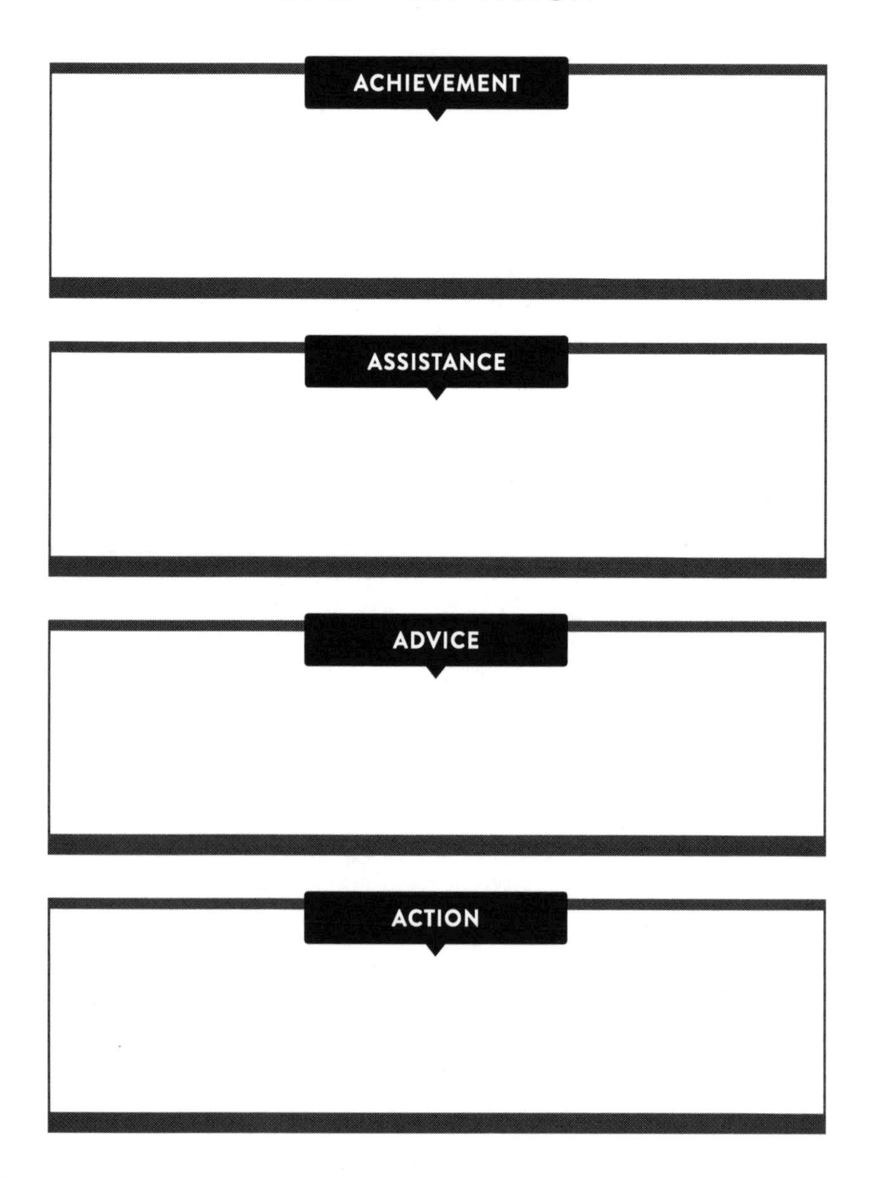

YOU ARE NEVER TOO SMALL TO BE BIG. BUT, ARE YOU READY TO LEAD?

ACT NOW ON THE 18 STRATEGIC STEPS AND BE THE LEADER OTHERS WILL ADMIRE AND FOLLOW.

MOUSETRAP MILESTONES

LEADERSHIP LESSONS	LEADER'S METAPHORS
Ownership	Broken Chair
Confidence	Cake
Ideas	Island-Mainland
Network	Well
Collaboration	Team of Rivals
Ideation	Intelligent Machines
Diversity	Palm
Empathy	Shoes
Prioritisation	Chicken or Egg
Focus	Mountain
Change	Sail
Trust	T-Cycle
Kingmakers	Random Walk or Guided Run
T.I.M.E.	Little Flower
Safety	Seat Belt
Resilience	Basketball
Trends	Shadow
Vision	Binoculars

FIND THE MOUSETRAPS IN YOUR HOUSE™

In your department, in your organisation, or in your team, you will always have some problems. Those are the 'Mousetraps in your house'. Some of these are Mousetraps that everyone knows about and chooses to ignore.

When my team and I conduct in-house leadership workshops for organisations, we help teams to internalise the mousetrap concept. This is done by getting them to take part in experiential learning activities, case study reviews, and brainstorming.

When we simulate an environment that encourages ownership, ideation, focus, productivity, diversity, empathy, communication and collaboration, participants open up and provide invaluable insights. This deepens awareness and learning. Such insights highlight the importance of thinking outside of our brains. This uncovers the in-house Mousetraps and helps to formulate strategic initiatives, tactical interventions and operational alignment.

WHAT'S NEXT?

You have by now read all chapters and hopefully completed the exercises at the end of each chapter. The questions posed to you at the end of each chapter were designed to engage you to think critically about your opportunities and challenges. What's next?

USING YOUR FREE MOUSETRAP REALITY CHECK TOOL

Sometimes we need an honest reality check on ourselves to see how far we have come, where we are and what we can aim for. This self-awareness is the foundation to be a leader others will admire and follow. The *Mousetrap Reality Check Tool* is designed to assess where you are on your leadership journey in relation to the environment you operate. You will be able to see how others perceive you, providing you with insights on what behaviours you have to repeat and blind spots you need to notice. Many participants were surprised to note that they had leadership competencies they didn't realise, but were valued greatly by others.

YOUR MOUSETRAP PACT

The *Mousetrap Pact* steps you prepared for each chapter will now become your *Pact.* This is your personal contract with yourself which signifies your promise and commitment to enhance your leadership competencies. Ownership is a habit that leads to leadership. Be accountable for your own personal development as nobody else will get more interested in this than you. Work with your Accountability partner, coach and kingmakers to review your plans at least once every month. You might see yourself redoing the *Mousetrap Pact* regularly to monitor your progress.

To get immediate tangible results, you need to work toward achieving your plan through conscious, deliberate and determined effort.

FREE RESOURCES FOR YOU

- ✓ Recommended reading list that deepens your learning and understanding.
- ✓ Download fresh copies of the Mousetrap Pact for repeated use.
- ✓ Download fresh copies of Mousetrap Reality Check Tool for repeated use.
- ✓ Read Articles from thought-leaders with tips, techniques and case studies.
- ✓ Watch Videos with innovative ideas and invaluable insights.
- ✓ Learn to PRIME your audience. PRIME=Persuade Resonate Inspire Mesmerize Entertain. Read well researched and time-tested tips you can put to use immediately.
- ✓ Posters, Quotes and Slides you can use for internal team meetings and seminars.

Visit Mousetrap Resource Centre at:

www.thoughtexpressions.com/mousetraponline

PLAN YOUR IMMEDIATE NEXT STEP

YOUR ROLE	YOUR NEXT STEP
If you are a CEO or head of department	Share the book, story, and lessons with your teams and ask them to prepare their *Mousetrap Pact.* This will ensure personal ownership, responsibility and accountability in addition to identifying the real needs of your team members. In our experience with many organisations, we have seen that this indirectly increases employee engagement.
If you are a senior executive or HR manager	Share the book, story, and lessons with your peers, superiors, and subordinates. Arrange a sharing session to discuss the lessons and help your team prepare their *Mousetrap Pacts.* In addition to that, you can choose to request the **Find The Mousetraps In Your House™** workshop for your team. My team and I can help you to conduct these sessions with case studies and experiential activities customised for your organisation.
If you are an employee or business owner	Prepare your *Mousetrap Pact.* Identify the opportunities you have and challenges you face. Believe in yourself and believe that you are never too small to be big. Make a conscious effort to master the various competencies you need to become a leader others choose to follow. You can also consider enrolling for the **Leaders By Design Bootcamp™**, to take stock of your current situation, find obstacles, and prepare workable plans for your personal mastery.

If you are a parent or teacher or mentor	Share the book, story, and lessons with your children, students and clients. Help them prepare their *Mousetrap Pact.* Help them to take ownership and accountability for their personal development.
If you are a student	Share the book, story, and lessons with your friends. Prepare your *Mousetrap Pact.* Identify the opportunities you have and the challenges you face. Believe in yourself and believe you are never too small to be big. Make a conscious, deliberate and determined effort to master the various skills you need to become a leader others choose to follow. The earlier you do this, the better prepared you will be for your future.

ACKNOWLEDGMENTS

I have been fortunate to have received immense help, support, and encouragement from many people without which this book would not have seen the light of day. I am grateful to all my mentors and well-wishers who regularly see in me what I do not see in myself.

I would also like to thank my father and my mother. Even though, both of them are not with us now, they still positively influence the way I think, speak, and behave, every single day.

My interest in leadership and leadership coaching came from my dear wife, Sindu. She once inspired me to leverage on my international experience in multinational companies in multiple countries to help others become better leaders. She rightly believes that many people in the world could achieve much more in life, if they had the right mentors, guides, and role models. Sindu continues to be a guiding light, an inspiration, a tough critic, and above all, a loving partner. To my son, Advaith, and daughter, Aditi, who blindly believe I am the best dad in the world. They invoke in me a heightened sense of ownership for their wellbeing. I constantly strive to be a good mentor and role model for them. Their relentless encouragement is what keeps me ticking. Thanks to my sister Manju, my brother Manesh, and their families for their sustained moral and emotional support.

The versatile Sandeep Mohan provided me with constant nudging and encouragement to make me complete this book. I am grateful that he agreed to illustrate the first edition of this book and produced stunning illustrations that capture the essence of each scene. He further gave me honest feedback to improve the manuscript and pushed me to excellence. I am also grateful to my friends Avi Liran and Lim Chee Hoo, who saw value in this book and encouraged me consistently to complete the manuscript.

Thanks to Carolyn Street-Johns, Low Kim Heng, and Mani Sujathan for allowing me to ask them a series of "quick-questions" in the course of writing this book. I am immensely grateful to the readers of the first edition who encouraged me to continue. Among them, I would like to particularly thank Steve Walker, Todd Hutchinson, Richard Ong and Aung Pye Tun. I am grateful to my editor Gwen Ling, for her professionalism, positive attitude and speedy responses. I would like to thank my art director and designer Wee Peng for the professional work and patience that went into designing this edition.

My father once told me, "*The big trees, you see here today were not planted by you or by me. They were planted by people who died long ago. Likewise, our job is not to worry about the result or the reward of our contributions. Our job is to do the best we can, to do something, that will someday, benefit someone.*" I sincerely hope this book will continue to benefit its readers and make them leaders who can lead movements that help humanity.

You, the Reader: If you have benefited from this book or if you have comments, suggestions, or insightful anecdotes that can be included in the next edition of the book, please write to our team at ***mousetrap@thoughtexpressions.com***. I would be grateful to you for every valuable input you provide and if it is adopted, we will acknowledge your contribution in the next edition of the book.

DETECT THE MOUSETRAPS IN YOUR HOUSE™

Facilitated Brainstorming and Ideation
Detect issues in your teams that are going unnoticed
Identify barriers to collaboration and productivity

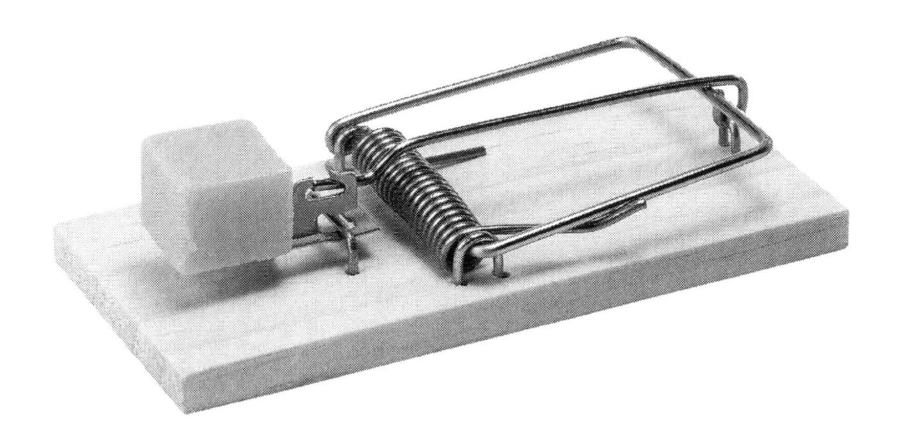

FORMULATE
Strategic Initiatives
Tactical Interventions
Operational Alignment

thoughtexpressions.com/mousetraponline

WORLD CLASS PERSONAL MASTERY AND LEADERSHIP EXCELLENCE

7 MOST POPULAR EXECUTIVE EDUCATION PROGRAMS OF THOUGHT EXPRESSIONS

1. Leadership Mastery Program™
2. Personal Mastery Program™
3. Executive Transformation Program™
4. Collaborative Creativity Program™
5. Corporate Storytelling Program™
6. Accelerated Speaking Program™
7. Leader By Design Bootcamp™

World-class high-impact transformative coaching sessions designed for:

- ✓ Personal mastery and leadership excellence.
- ✓ Increase self-awareness, ownership and collaboration.
- ✓ Master the management of stress, conflicts, politics and change.
- ✓ Increase focus, creativity and productivity.
- ✓ Win with people by mastering the Power of 5. Learn to connect, communicate, network, lead and sell.
- ✓ Resonate. Captivate. Inspire. Convince.
- ✓ Build a class of best performers at all levels.

For a complete list of our worldwide programs and services, please visit **www.ThoughtExpressions.com**

LEADERS™ BY DESIGN BOOTCAMP

Enable your team for Ownership and Personal mastery

Enhance collaboration and team work

Reduce conflicts, increase productivity and profitability

More details at:

thought expressions

www.ThoughtExpressions.com/ mousetraponline

WOULD YOU LIKE TO BE REMEMBERED FOR YOUR MESSAGES?

Learn to **PRIME** your audience

PRIME = **P**ersuade **R**esonate **I**nspire **M**esmerize **E**ntertain.
Well-researched. Time-tested. FREE.

Get your free PRIME tips at
www.ThoughtExpressions.com

EXECUTIVE TRANSFORMATION PROGRAM™

Make your teams work wonders.

HIGH-IMPACT GROUP COACHING SESSIONS OVER 6 MONTHS DESIGNED FOR TEAM EXCELLENCE

More information at
www.ThoughtExpressions.com

ACCELERATED™
SPEAKING
PROGRAM
Dramatically improve your confidence, presentation & speaking skills!
Participate in LIVE sessions in-person or from anywhere in the world.
Don't be stuck with average speaking skills.
Cut off years from your learning curve.
High-impact live coaching sessions over 5 weeks.
Designed for your transformation.
thought
expressions
Details and Testimonials at:
ThoughtExpressions.com/asp

NEED HELP? REACH OUT!

GET COACHED BY

MANOJ VASUDEVAN

Executive Coaching
Leadership Coaching
Public Speaking Coaching
Corporate Storytelling Coaching

1 on 1

Face-to-face or remotely
anywhere in the world

thought
expressions

www.ThoughtExpressions.com/1-on-1

MOST POPULAR MOUSETRAP QUOTES

1. You are never too small to be big.
2. Ownership is the habit that leads to leadership.
3. In a team, somebody's problem is everybody's problem.
4. Don't give excuses. Give excellence.
5. Competence is important. Confidence is paramount.
6. The person with greater confidence has the upper hand.
7. Generating ideas isn't enough. Infuse ideas.
8. Don't just tell or yell, sell!
9. Dig your wells and build your bridges long before you need them.
10. Collaboration is common sense. But, collaboration is not common.
11. You don't have to agree with a person completely to work with them. Tolerate. Cooperate. Operate.
12. Ideation is the foundation of creation.
13. Think outside your brain.
14. We should no longer feel the pressure to know everything, even in our domain of expertise.
15. Diversity is your reality. Embrace diversity before it is too late.
16. Ego is the enemy of empathy.
17. We can't solve everyone's problems. But, we can help them feel better and get ahead.
18. What should come first, the Chicken or the Egg?

19. Prioritisation should be your first priority.
20. Even if you have 1000 things to do, there will only be 24 hours a day. Prioritise.
21. Focus accelerates progress.
22. Change happens with 5 constants. Expect. Adapt. Adjust. Adopt. Accept.
23. Demonstrate that you are committed to carry out the change.
24. Trust is built by effort and demolished by stupidity.
25. People are consistently looking for clues about whether or not you are trustworthy.
26. What is consistent is trusted. What is inconsistent is doubted.
27. Every king is surrounded by kingmakers.
28. Mentors can help you be the best you by bringing out the best in you.
29. Look for the best people and look for the best in people.
30. Are you doing a Random Walk or a Guided Run?
31. Purpose provides meaning to life.
32. Safety is your best insurance policy.
33. The only mistake is to be afraid to make more mistakes.
34. Resilience is the refusal to be paralysed by failures.
35. Let go of the setbacks and look forward to the bounce backs. Hope is what keeps the dream alive.
36. Be aware of what's coming your way.
37. Size matters. The size of your dreams matters.

AN IDEAL GIFT

For members of your organisation.

Rational, inspirational and easy-to-implement strategic steps toward personal mastery and leadership.

A game plan for the future.

Discover the game plan every employee, employer, parent, student, and teacher needs to know.

For bulk orders: books@asmanyminds.com

ABOUT MANOJ VASUDEVAN

(PRONOUNCED MA-NOĴ WA-SU-DEV-AN)

Manoj is an internationally respected leadership coach, management consultant and communications expert. He holds an MBA from Imperial College London. Manoj has over 21 years experience with many major MNC clients in Asia, Australia, USA and Europe. He has coached individuals from 27 nationalities including C-Level Executives, Senior Executives, Bureaucrats, Management Consultants, Celebrities, UN diplomats, Sales Teams and professionals.

Manoj is currently the CEO of Thought Expressions and the Managing director of XB5 Consulting. In 2015, Manoj was crowned World Number Three at the World Championship of Public Speaking Las Vegas, ranking him amongst the top three competitive speakers worldwide among a pool of 35,000 aspirants from 135 countries. Manoj has spoken in several cities across the world with sessions that are eye-opening, engaging, energizing and entertaining.

Manoj is also the co-author of the Amazon #1 Bestseller in Public Speaking "World Class Speaking in Action" and the author of "Nervous to Fabulous: 7 steps to mastery in any field of your choice".

 sg.linkedin.com/in/manojthecoach

 facebook.com/manojthecoach/

 twitter.com/vsmanoj

Write to us at
talk2us@thoughtexpressions.com